DOSTOEVSKY

FYODOR MIKHAILOVITCH DOSTOEVSKY

by V. G. Perov (1878)

DOSTOEVSKY

A STUDY

by

JANKO LAVRIN

WITH A PORTRAIT FRONTISPIECE

NEW YORK / RUSSELL & RUSSELL

FIRST PUBLISHED, 1943, BY METHUEN & COMPANY LIMITED, LONDON

COPYRIGHT, 1947, BY JANKO LAVRIN

REISSUED, 1969, BY RUSSELL & RUSSELL

A DIVISION OF ATHENEUM PUBLISHERS, INC.

BY ARRANGEMENT WITH JANKO LAVRIN

L. C. CATALOG CARD NO: 68-27069

PRINTED IN THE UNITED STATES OF AMERICA

A PREFATORY NOTE

THE substance of the present study is based on my book, *Dostoevsky and his Creation*, which has now been out of print for a number of years. The entire matter has been so much revised and rewritten that, to all intents and purposes, this study can be regarded as a new work, more or less adapted to the present historical moment. The quotations used are mainly from Mrs. Garnett's translation of Dostoevsky's works (Heinemann). For several passages I am indebted to *Letters of F. M. Dostoevsky*, translated by Colburn Mayne (Chatto and Windus), to *Stavrogin's Confession*, translated by S. Koteliansky (Hogarth Press), and to *Pages from the Journal of an Author*, translated by S. Koteliansky and J. M. Mury (Maunsel & Co.). To the publishers of all these works my sincere thanks are due. In a few instances the translations are my own.

J. L.

CONTENTS

DOSTOEVSKY

I

SOME NOTES ON DOSTOEVSKY'S LIFE

I

ONE is tempted to regard as symbolic the fact that Fyodor Mikhailovitch Dostoevsky was born, on October 30th 1821, in a Moscow hospital for the poor, where his father was employed as a physician. As the Dostoevsky family occupied a flat in the hospital buildings, some of the boy's earliest impressions were those of pain, poverty and disease. In spite of the patriarchal atmosphere prevailing in his family, the old Dostoevsky—an offspring of the impoverished gentry—was of an irritable disposition, miserly and addicted to drink. He had a miserable end. Having bought a small farm in the Tula district, he treated his few serfs so badly that in the end they murdered him, in 1838.

Fyodor was first educated in Moscow, and then in Petersburg at the College of Military Engineering. Feeling isolated among his richer and less developed comrades, he found a refuge in reading. He greedily read all the authors, Russian and foreign, that were in vogue at the time: Gogol, Pushkin, Balzac, Hoffmann, George Sand, Eugène Sue, Victor Hugo, and later also Dickens. Most of these writers exercised some influence on Dostoevsky's budding genius, especially Balzac, Hoffmann and Gogol. Balzac (whose *Eugénie Grandet* he translated into Russian) fostered his own capacity for intensifying characters into 'maniacs', while Hoffmann and Gogol appealed to him by their grotesque mixture of reality and fantasy. A favourite of his was also Friedrich Schiller, whom he later ridiculed and used as a nickname for naïve enthusiasts.

To these romantic and semi-romantic influences the

early examples of the Russian 'natural school' should be added. Its initiator was Gogol, but its chief advocate was the critic Belinsky, who demanded from literature truth to life and service to humanitarian ideals. A strong imprint upon Dostoevsky's literary work was, however, left by Petersburg itself. Behind the colossal, externally cold and prosaic metropolis of Russia he soon perceived a phantomlike city: the most 'abstract' city on earth. During the winter evenings, and also during the magical white nights in the early summer, Petersburg must often have seemed to him a *fata morgana*, conjured up among the Finnish marshes in order to disappear at the first cock-crow in the morning. In contrast to the bright, clearly defined colours of the southern towns, here everything was half-tone in a misty haze. And behind the architectural masses, delineated against a low sleepy sky, one suspected another reality, until each corner, each figure began to look different from what it was: spectral, nightmarish, and yet curiously real.

This feature of Petersburg appealed to certain mental and artistic propensities of Dostoevsky himself. Several years later (1861) he described one of his early impressions of the Russian capital in the following terms: 'I remember, once in the wintry month of January, I was hurrying home. I was still very young. As I drew near to the Neva, I stopped for a moment and looked along the river into the hazy frost-dim distance which suddenly glowed with the last purple flash of the evening, while fading away on the horizon. The night was settling down, and over the snowy plain of the Neva myriads of sparks from the misty rime were spread by the last gleam of the sun. It was very cold. . . . A chilly vapour rose from the tired horses, from the hurrying passers-by. The dense air trembled at the slightest sound, and from all the roofs there rolled pillars of smoke across the cold sky—rolled mingling and scattering on their way, so that it seemed new buildings were mounting above the old ones, and a new city was being pieced together in the air. . . . At last I had the impression as though the whole of that realm with its inhabitants, houses, dens of beggary, and gilded palaces, were but a fantastic magical vision, a dream, which in its turn would disappear and dissolve in the dark-blue sky. A strange idea stirred within me. I shivered and felt the thrill of a mighty hitherto unknown emotion. My mind caught as it were something which until then had been hidden in me like a vague foreboding; my gaze penetrated into a new world, of which I had had no idea before—but for a few of its mysterious hints and tokens. And from then on, that is, from that vision of mine (for I call my experience on the Neva a vision) exceedingly strange things began to happen to me.'

His childhood and adolescence in Moscow, and his subsequent stay in Petersburg, explain why Dostoevsky became predominantly a novelist of the city—as distinct from the manor novelists, typical of the great period of Russian realism. Even the rapid pace of his novels, so different from the leisurely tempo of Tolstoy, Turgenev or Goncharov, reminds one of the hectic town life. At the same time, it would be almost impossible to dissociate Dostoevsky's works from the 'psychic' atmosphere of Petersburg. This applies even to those narratives the action of which takes place in the provinces.

II

On leaving college, Dostoevsky obtained a commission, but he soon resigned and decided—somewhat rashly—to live by literature. It was under the influence of Gogol's *The Cloak* that he wrote—in the old-fashioned letter form —his first short novel, *Poor Folk*. This story of platonic love on the part of an elderly copying clerk for an orphan girl may bear traces of Gogol, yet its psychology is remarkable. So is the author's subtlety of approach. The MS. was shown in May 1845 to the poet Nekrasov, who passed it on to Belinsky. Both were stirred to admiration.

Belinsky, who saw in this narrative a humanitarian social novel, took the young debutant under his wing, and Dostoevsky became known in literary circles even before *Poor Folk* was published, in January 1846. This sudden popularity was, however, too much for him. Some of his letters of that period are full of a childish swagger.

'Well, brother,' he wrote in one of them to his brother Michael, 'I believe that my fame is just now in its fullest flower. Everywhere I meet with the most amazing consideration and enormous interest. I have made the acquaintance of a lot of very important people. Prince Odoyevsky[1] begs me for the honour of a visit, and Count Sollogub[2] is tearing his hair in desperation. Panayev[3] told him that a new genius had arisen who would sweep all the rest away. . . . Everybody looks upon me as a wonder of the world. If I but open my mouth, the air resounds with what Dostoevsky means to do. Belinsky loves me unboundedly. The writer Turgenev, who has just returned from Paris, has from the first been more than friendly, and Belinsky declared that Turgenev has quite lost his heart to me. . . . All the Minnas, Claras, Mariannas, etc., have got amazingly pretty, but cost a lot of money. Turgenev and Belinsky lately gave me a talking-to about my disorderly way of life.'

In the meantime Dostoevsky's second long story, *The Double*, was a failure. Here, too, he was under Gogol's influence.[4] Gogol's *Memoirs of a Madman*, and even more his grotesque *The Nose*, together with E. T. A. Hoffmann's *Die Elixiere des Teufels* (The Devil's Elixirs), must have inspired his main theme: the split personality. *The Double* is, for a young author, an unusually

[1] A representative of Russian romanticism who was under German influence.

[2] A well-known author of that period.

[3] The co-editor of *Sovremennik* (The Contemporary) which he and the poet Nekrasov bought in 1846.

[4] Readers interested in the part played by Gogol in Russian literature can consult my book, *An Introduction to the Russian Novel* (Methuen).

penetrating work; a disguised self-analysis in fact, a confession. It is deeper than *Poor Folk*. But the literary lawgiver Belinsky sealed its fate by labelling it 'pathologic rubbish'. Misunderstandings with Belinsky increased also because Dostoevsky had joined the staff of the *Fatherland's Annals* with which Belinsky and Nekrasov had severed all contact.

Poor Folk and *The Double* betray, as it were, the two main trends of Dostoevsky's later and more important writings. In the first of them he is drawn towards the 'insulted and injured'. And in the second he describes the subconscious reactions of a crushed but secretly rebellious personality with an intuition amounting to clairvoyance. On the whole, the first two years of his literary career show curious ups and downs. He wrote during that time about a dozen stories—uneven, but always testifying to that uncanny psychological vein which later secured him a unique place in world literature. In *The Landlady* (a story, influenced by Gogol's *Terrible Vengeance*) Dostoevsky's psychological propensity touches upon caricature, but he makes up for it by his unfinished novel, *Netochka Nezvanova*. This work is above all an analysis of a self-centred and 'injured' orphan child, brought up in utter misery and later adopted by an aristocrat whose capricious daughter first maltreats her with sadistic gusto, but gradually becomes passionately attached to her.

Dostoevsky was hard at work upon this intense if confused novel, when a sudden catastrophe intervened. On April 23rd, 1849, he was arrested as a member of the revolutionary Petrashevsky circle (consisting of youths interested, above all, in the socialist theories of Fourier). While awaiting the trial, he wrote in the dungeon *A Little Hero*, one of his serenest short stories, analysing the erotic awakening in a boy. Before Christmas of the same year the first truly dramatic climax of his life took place. Together with twenty other condemned members of the circle he was conveyed to a square on which there was a scaffold. But let us listen to Dostoevsky's own words: 'To-day, the 22nd of December,' he wrote to his brother, 'we were all taken to the Semyonovsky Square. There the death sentence was read to us, we were given the cross to kiss, the dagger was broken over our heads, and our funeral toilet (white shirts) was made. Then three of us were put standing before the palisades for the execution of the death sentence. I was sixth in the row; we were called up by groups of three and so I was in the second group and had not more than a minute to live. . . . I had time to embrace Pleshcheiev and Durov, who stood near me, and to take my leave of them. Finally, the retreat was sounded, those who were bound to the palisades were brought back, and it was read to us that "His Imperial Majesty had granted us our lives".'

During this abject performance one of the condemned went mad and never recovered. As for Dostoevsky, he passed in those few minutes through the terrible experiences to which he often referred in his writings (above all in *The Idiot*). To put a final touch to the procedure, the rebels were sent in chains, almost straight from the scaffold, to Siberia.

III

However brief Dostoevsky's revolutionary activities may have been, they are of interest on account of his later views and attitudes. Petrashevsky himself was an insignificant, even irresponsible personality. As for his associates, the majority of them were harmless individuals, carried away by the liberal ideas of 1848, as well as by the Utopian French socialism of those days. Circles of liberal-minded theoreticians and talkers became quite a tradition in Russia after the Napoleonic campaigns. The most notable among them were the 'Decembrists' whose ringleaders were executed after the rising of December 1825—a rising which, by the way, forms a landmark in the cultural destinies of modern Russia. For

it was after 1825 that the guardianship of Russian civilization gradually began to pass from the educated nobility
to a new and more or less classless body: the intelligentsia
whose formation began in the thirties of the last century.
The intelligentsia proper was a blend of liberal members of the gentry on the one hand and of educated
commoners or *raznochintsy* (people of no rank) on the
other. Imbued with the advanced ideas of the West, the
Russian intellectuals were anxious, at the very outset, to
rid their country of autocracy and of serfdom, although
for years they had to be contented with mere theories.
Yet they put into those theories all their moral indignation
and idealistic temper. Belinsky—a commoner by birth—
was the most outstanding leader the intelligentsia in its
early stages was able to produce. And the personality of
Belinsky left an unmistakable mark in the mind and—
indirectly—even in the work of Dostoevsky.

First of all, it was Belinsky to whom he was largely
indebted for his brilliant literary debut. Secondly,
Belinsky's idealistic 'fury' corresponded to something
similar in Dostoevsky who was unable to stop half-way
in anything. Hence the more he had been drawn towards
Belinsky during the *Poor Folk* vogue, the more did he
soon resent the critic's scathing opinion of *The Double*,
not to mention certain other purely personal misunderstandings. Indeed, his resentment against Belinsky was
eventually directed well-nigh against everything Belinsky
stood for. For the time being he remained of course under
the sway of the progressive ideas of the Petrashevsky
circle, or rather of those of his generation, however much
the latter were at variance with the patriarchal religious
atmosphere of his early upbringing. But the actual conflict between his inherited religious propensities on the
one hand and his reasoned out ideas on the other, came
to a head during and after his Siberian experiences. As a
consequence, his views and convictions underwent a total
change.

Once such a 'conversion' had taken place in him, the Belinsky type of intellectual—a votary of science and rationalism—was bound to become his *bête noire*. So much so that whenever, in his later years, Dostoevsky wrote with bitterness about the Russian radicals, one could almost invariably detect in the background the shadow of Belinsky. Yet during his Petrashevsky period Dostoevsky must have been as impetuous a liberal as any member of that circle. It was he who had read aloud, at one of the gatherings, Belinsky's famous letter to Gogol —a letter full of bitter attacks on obscurantism, autocracy, serfdom, and the official Church. Moreover, he was among those few members who had dared to set up a secret printing press with the purpose of broadcasting revolutionary propaganda. Fortunately, this was not discovered by the tribunal, investigating his case, otherwise Tsar Nicholas I would hardly have contented himself with staging a mock execution. Among the members primarily responsible for the press were, as far as can be gathered, Dostoevsky and a strange individual, called Speshnyov.

Speshnyov was a polished aristocrat and a cynic with an enormous will-power which he used for purely destructive purposes. Yet his irony and devastating radicalism seemed to be only a mask for his own inner desolation. His very face resembled a mask, at once fascinating and repellent. No wonder that Dostoevsky, with his flair for everything out of the ordinary, succumbed to the power of that character in whose cold Mephistophelian mockery he probably found a tonic against the 'Schilleresque' exaltation he himself was prone to indulge in at that period. At the same time, he must have feared and hated Speshnyov's intellectual daring in so far as he probably sensed in it destructive promptings similar to those which lurked in the hidden recesses of his own nature. Nor was he perhaps unaware that Speshnyov's nihilism was but the final conclusion of certain ideas, disseminated by the well-meaning liberal Belinsky and adhered to by the members of the Petrashevsky circle, himself included. In any case, this suspicion continued to trouble him and manifested itself much later in one of his most formidable novels, *The Possessed*, whose chief character, Stavrogin, is a partial portrait of Speshnyov. Also a few other pre-Siberian reminiscences and impressions can be traced in Dostoevsky's later works.

IV

In Siberia Dostoevsky spent four years in the company of murderers, robbers and other criminals from all parts of Russia. 'I had made acquaintance with convicts in Tobolsk,' he wrote later (in 1854) to his brother, 'at Omsk I settled myself down to live four years with them. They are rough, angry, embittered men. Their hatred for the nobility is boundless; they regard all of us who belong to it with hostility and enmity. They would have devoured us if only they could. Judge then for yourself in what danger we stood, having to share our lives with these people for some years, eat with them, sleep by them, and with no possibility of complaining of the affronts which were constantly put upon us. . . . A hundred and fifty foes never wearied of persecuting—it was their joy, their diversion, their pastime; our sole shield was our indifference and our moral superiority, which they were forced to recognize and respect.'

And this is how he describes to his brother the atmosphere of the penal settlement at Omsk in which he lived all those years—burdened with chains, and subject to the same treatment as the most hardened criminals: 'Imagine an old, crazy, wooden building, that should long ago have been broken up as useless. In the summer it is unbearably hot, in the winter it is unbearably cold. All the boards are rotten; on the ground filth lies an inch thick; every instant one is in danger of slipping and coming down. The small windows are so frozen over that even by day one can scarcely read. The ice on the panes is three

inches thick. The ceilings drip, there are draughts everywhere. We are packed like herrings in a barrel. The
stove is heated with six logs of wood, but the room is so
cold that the ice never thaws; the atmosphere is unbearable—and so the whole winter. In the same room the
prisoners wash their linen, and thus make the place so
wet that one dare scarcely move. From twilight till
morning we are forbidden to leave the barrack-room; the
doors are barricaded; in the ante-room a great wooden
trough for the calls of nature is placed; this makes one
hardly able to breathe. All the prisoners stink like pigs;
they say they can't help it, for they must live, and are but
men. We slept upon bare boards; each man was allowed
one pillow only. We covered ourselves with sheepskins,
and our feet were outside the covering all the time. It
was thus we froze night after night. Fleas, lice, and other
vermin by the bushel. In the winter we got thin sheepskins to wear, which didn't keep us warm at all, and
short-legged boots. Thus equipped, we had to go out
into the frost.'

After his brief spell of fame and success, Dostoevsky
was buried alive in that hell where his personality was
constantly humiliated and crushed. His only solace was
a copy of the New Testament, given to him in Tobolsk
by one of those heroic wives who had followed their
husbands, the participants of the 'Decembrist' rising of
1825, to Siberia. Fortunately for literature, Dostoevsky
turned even penal servitude to advantage. In the quoted
letter he remarks: 'I won't even try to tell you what
transformations were undergone by my soul, my faith,
my mind, and my heart, in those four years. It would be
a long story. Still, the eternal concentration, the escape
into myself from bitter reality, did bear its fruit. I have
now needs and hopes of which I never thought in other
days. But all this will be pure enigma to you, and so I'll
pass on to other things.'

It is beyond doubt that the criminals he became

familiar with must have revolutionized Dostoevsky's former ideas of good and evil. The germs of a brooding 'transvaluer' are to be sought in some of his experiences in the *katorga* (penal settlement) where he could watch human nature divested of all its masks and disguises. The enigma of man and of the irrational human self appeared, under those conditions, in so many new aspects that on leaving this 'house of the dead', Dostoevsky was a different human being from the one who had entered it four years earlier.

After his release he was sent as a private to a Siberian line-battalion, stationed at Semipalatinsk, in which he served another five years. Here he found an influential friend in the young baron Wrangel and fell, moreover, in love with Mme Isayeva, the wife of a minor customs official. Hysterical, irresponsible and with a streak of cruelty, she yet possessed a certain charm which proved irresistible to the erotically starved ex-convict. Her sick husband was soon transferred to another town where he died. As Dostoevsky had been promoted, meanwhile, to a commissioned rank, the widow summoned him to her new place (Kuznetsk), and the two were married. She had a lover at the time—an impecunious teacher—whom Dostoevsky befriended: a situation, described by him in *The Insulted and Injured*, and anticipated as it were in his youthful *White Nights*. An unreliable rumour would have it that she had spent the night before the wedding with her lover whom she is also supposed to have supported subsequently for some seven years.

Three years after his marriage, Dostoevsky was allowed to return to European Russia. He settled down with his wife and his stepson first in Tver and a few months later in Petersburg, where he resumed his literary activities with a new zest and a new outlook upon life. Curiously enough, the first two narratives he contributed to literature after this long interval have nothing to do with his Siberian experiences, although he wrote them while still in Siberia (1859). Both of them may be regarded as a humorous refuge in which traces of Gogol and also of Dickens are noticeable. Of the two stories the boisterously funny short novel, *The Village Stepanchikovo* (1859), is better than the ironical *Uncle's Dream* (1859). Its chief character, Foma Opiskin, is a well-portrayed Russian Tartuffe (or rather Pecksniff). At the same time he is a frustrated individual who takes revenge for his crushed self by trying to tyrannize every one around him as soon as he feels power in his hands. The events lead, quite unexpectedly, to a comic denouement in which all ends well. But, in spite of such an ending, the aggressive parasite Foma forestalls some of Dostoevsky's more sinister heroes. The characterization wavers between humour and satire —a method which he brought to great perfection in *An Unpleasant Predicament* (1862) and in some of his later portraits, especially in Stepan Trofimovich (*The Possessed*).

Dostoevsky's only work dealing with convict life is his *Memoirs of the House of the Dead* (1861)—one of the most powerful autobiographic and psychological documents. What enhances the effect of this work is its understatement. Dostoevsky never dramatizes himself and his suffering. The greatest horrors of the *katorga* are described in a calm matter-of-fact tone. Not only does he extend broad human sympathy to his fellow convicts, but he has good words even for some of his jailers. In many criminal outcasts he actually discovered 'deep, strong, beautiful natures', gone astray through no fault of their own. 'How much joyless youth,' he concludes, 'how much strength for which use there was none, was buried, lost in those walls!—youth and strength of which the world might surely have made *some* use. For I must speak my thought as to this: the hapless fellows there were perhaps the strongest and, in one way or another, the most gifted of our people. There was all that strength of body and mind lost. Whose fault is that?'

It was this new attitude towards the criminal that made

Friedrich Nietzsche write, several years later, in his *Twilight of the Idols*: 'The criminal type is the type of strong man made sick. . . . Concerning the problem before us, Dostoevsky's testimony is of importance. Dostoevsky, who, incidentally, was the only psychologist from whom I had anything to learn: he belongs to the happiest windfalls of my life, happier even than the discovery of Stendhal. This profound man, who was right ten times over in esteeming the superficial Germans low, found the Siberian convicts among whom he lived—those thoroughly hopeless criminals for whom no road back to society stood open—very different from what even he had expected—that is to say, carved from about the best, hardest and most valuable material that grows on Russian soil.'

Dostoevsky may not refer to the *katorga* in his stories and novels. Yet there is no doubt that the years he had spent there must have had a decisive influence upon his life and work: they gave a new trend to both. It was in Siberia that he had plunged into that psychic and spiritual 'underworld' which played such an important part in the whole of his post-Siberian work. Only a man who had passed through the trials described in *The House of the Dead* could have become so acutely alive to the significance—social and metaphysical—of the human self as Dostoevsky. This work does not stand apart from his writings as some critics would have it. On the contrary, it explains, at least indirectly, his principal themes and attitudes.

Of considerable importance also was his 'sacred disease' or epilepsy which had been latent in him since boyhood, but attacked him seriously in Siberia, never to leave him again. The 'Dickensian' Nellie in *The Insulted and Injured*, Prince Myshkin in *The Idiot*, Kirillov in *The Possessed*, Smerdyakov in *The Brothers Karamozov* are typical epileptics. Yet it was not the clinical side of this disease that Dostoevsky was interested in, but the ineffable spiritual exaltation preceding the fits—a state of consciousness he knew from personal experience. This is how Kirillov describes it:

'There are seconds—they come five or six at a time—when you suddenly feel the presence of the eternal harmony perfectly attained. It's something not earthly—I don't mean in the sense that it is heavenly—but in the sense that man cannot endure it in his earthly aspect. He must be physically changed or˙die. This feeling is clear and unmistakable; it's as though you apprehend all nature and suddenly you say, "Yes, that's right." God, when He created the world, said at the end of each day of creation, "Yes, it's right, it's good." It . . . it's not being deeply moved, but simply joy. You don't forgive anything, because there's no need of forgiveness. It's not that you love—oh, there's in it something higher than love—what's most awful is that it's terribly clear and such joy. If it lasted more than five seconds the soul could not endure it and must perish. In those five seconds I live through a lifetime, and I'd give my whole life for them, because they are worth it. To endure ten seconds one must be physically changed.'

A man familiar with such states of consciousness was bound to ask himself, sooner or later, whether the 'eternal harmony' revealed by them was not mere delusion, and what lay beneath it all—a question which, in Dostoevsky's opinion, transcended the boundaries of mere psychology or pathology. Another aspect, connected with his epilepsy was the after-effect which proved as depressing as its approach had been ecstatic. According to his own statement, it consisted of an overpowering feeling of guilt: as though he had committed some crime which then kept on haunting him. Such experiences were bound to foster all the more Dostoevsky's interest in crime and in criminals.

Even his leanings towards the simple people and their mentality was largely due to the *katorga*. Born and bred in a big city, Dostoevsky had had scarcely any opportunity of thoroughly studying the Russian people. In Siberia, however, he came into direct contact with types from all parts of Russia. In spite of his aloofness and his initial disgust, he saw that the material out of which some of those convicts were made was good and full of possibilities, provided it was properly understood and handled. Gradually, the one-time revolutionary and town intellectual began to look for deeper organic ties with the Russian masses from which he hoped to draw a new vitality. He even concocted his own brand of 'populism', coinciding to some extent with the Slavophil worship of the *moujik*, but more complex and deeper than either the doctrines of the Slavophils or those of the populist radicals, so prevalent in the 'sixties and 'seventies.

V

On his return to Petersburg, Dostoevsky and his brother Michael started, in 1861, *Vremia* (The Time), a liberal periodical, but with a populist-religious tendency. Without bothering about ethnographic traditionalism, so dear to the Slavophils, he preached the need of overcoming the gap between the people and the intelligentsia (one of Russia's most vital problems) through an organic rootedness in the soil. In this doctrine he was joined by the philosopher Strakhov and by the poet and critic Apollon Grigoryev. In the same periodical he was groping for a reconciliation or even a synthesis between the nationalist Slavophils and the cosmopolitan Westerners—an idea which culminated, much later, in his famous Pushkin Speech of 1880.

Dostoevsky's gospel of 'rootedness' was perhaps an instinctive self-defence against the instability and the general 'flux' (whether mental, political or economic) in which he found Russia after the liberation of the serfs in 1861. Together with the old feudal order, the patriarchal forms of life were tumbling down. The intelligentsia, torn from the soil, from the people, and thrown back upon itself, had been even earlier a prey to isolation and a

Hamlet-like introspection. There was a topsy-turvydom
of values, of trends and ideas—a continually changing
stream which Dostoevsky began to explore, not only in its
temporary aspects, but also *sub specie aeternitatis*.

It was in *Vremia* that his novel, *The Insulted and
Injured* (1861) and his *Memoirs of the House of the Dead*
(1862) appeared. Yet one can hardly believe that these
two works were written by one and the same man. *The
House of the Dead* is a detached and intensely realistic
document, devoid of self-pity, as well as of any preaching
or moralizing. Certain passages—for example, the scene
of convicts in the bath—are unsurpassed in modern
literature. Memorable is also its psychological side,
notably the author's glimpses into the morbid self-
assertion of certain criminals. The novel, on the other
hand, expresses Dostoevsky's literary faults rather than
virtues. It is decidedly below his usual level, although it
contains interesting analytical passages. Its chief heroine,
Natasha, resembles some of the author's subsequent
characters. So does the self-divided Alyosha. Prince
Valkovski found a further development in Svidrigailov
(*Crime and Punishment*). The hysterical child, Nellie, is
reminiscent of Netochka, but at the same time anticipates
Liza in *The Brothers Karamazov*. Otherwise this novel
is badly constructed, long-drawn, garrulous and often
sentimental. It can hardly give one an idea of what
Dostoevsky's later and greater novels are like.

Little known is Dostoevsky's series of sketches, *Winter
Notes of Summer Impressions*, which were printed (1863)
in the same periodical. It is a lively journalistic account
of the author's first journey abroad in 1862. But a visit
to Paris, London, Geneva and Florence revealed to him
the incurably philistine character of Western civilization.
He felt as disappointed with its smug 'bourgeois' trend
as the ex-Westerner Alexander Herzen (whom he visited
in London) had felt before him. Spiritually, he regarded
the West as a corpse. In a chapter on London, under the

title, *Baal*, he gave a number of gruesome pictures of its bustling industrialism, its iniquities, and its sordid night-life. Whatever the literary value of these sketches may be, they throw much light on the author's mentality, especially on some of his basic ideas after Siberia.

In 1863 *Vremia* was suspended by the authorities because of an article on Polish affairs. This was a hard blow to Dostoevsky—a man utterly careless in matters of finance. As though to console himself, he borrowed some money and again went abroad. While in Wiesbaden, he gambled at the roulette table with a passion so well described a couple of years later in his absorbing but uneven short novel, *The Gambler*. This work is in fact autobiographical, at least in some of its aspects. The despotic 'granny' is believed to be a portrait of Dosto-evsky's wealthy aunt, whereas in the chief heroine Polina is portrayed a certain Apollinaria Suslova (a former con-tributor to *Vremia*) with whom he was in love at the time. Judging by her *Diary*, she must have been a capricious and hectic personality, endowed with a cruel strain which probably appealed to Dostoevsky whom she refused to treat as a man and a lover. During his second journey abroad, he found her in Paris with a lover who soon abandoned her. Her relationship towards Dostoevsky became more complicated and charged with that love-hate attitude which remained, from now on, one of his favourite motives.[1] Polina consented to travel with him in Germany, Switzerland and Italy. But in Baden-Baden Dostoevsky gambled again and, having lost his last penny, was forced to borrow from her even his train-fare to Petersburg.

Later both met again, but her attitude towards him was now chiefly one of hatred, as may be seen from some of the entries in her diary. Thus on December 14th,

---

[1] We find it in Nastasya (*The Idiot*), Liza (*The Possessed*), Kater-ina Ahmakova (*A Raw Youth*), and Katerina Ivanovna (*The Brothers Karamazov*).

1864, she wrote: 'When I remember what I was two years ago, I begin to hate D. (Dostoevsky). He was the first to kill all faith in me.' And on November 2nd, 1865: 'To-day we argued and contradicted each other for ever so long. For quite a time he has been offering his hand and heart to me, but he only annoys me. Speaking of my character he said: "If you ever marry, in three days you will hate your husband and run away from him. . . . You cannot forgive that once you gave yourself to me, and now you are taking your revenge for it; this is a woman's way."'

Dostoevsky's cult of self-humiliation, of love through hatred and of hatred through love, must have found particular gratification in his passion for Suslova. He never quite got rid of the spell she had cast over him and portrayed her (or at least her outstanding features) in a number of his women characters. As for Suslova, she married in 1880 the subsequently famous writer and authority on problems of sex, Vasily Rozanov, sixteen years her junior. She soon left him though, in a vindictive manner, without even granting him a divorce.[1]

Meanwhile Dostoevsky and his brother embarked in 1864 upon another less liberal periodical, *Epokha* (The Epoch). The venture was a financial failure. Its chief asset was that it brought out Dostoevsky's provocative *Notes from the Underworld*—a work the author wrote under most deplorable conditions in Moscow, in a room next to that of his dying wife. It may best be described as the soliloquy of a hopelessly battered human self. We also see in it for the first time Dostoevsky's power of dramatizing ideas. The whole of the first part is a philosophic expression of an 'underworld' attitude towards life, with the exphasis on the irrational. The hero, whose jeering at the world comes from wounded idealism,

---

[1] It appears rather paradoxical that Rozanov became one of the first and acutest commentators on Dostoevsky among the Russian modernists.

is a man with a paralysed will—paralysed by his own mental superiority and his overdeveloped sensitiveness. Having failed to become a 'success' in the scramble for existence, he is despised not only by the successful vulgarians who once happened to be his schoolfellows, but even by his ultra-respectable blockhead of a servant. As he is unable to assert his crushed ego in any other way, he asserts it through spite, nihilism and rancorous self-laceration. His cruelty to the prostitute, who comes to him as her saviour, is in essence but cruelty to himself—the cruelty of a man smashing his head against the wall. The 'inferiority complex' of a down-trodden individual with his secret but futile craving for a worthy, dignified life has rarely been expressed with such pitiless depth as in this work which provides a valuable clue to Dostoevsky's prepossessions and dilemmas. His hostility to all sorts of socialist trends became, from now on, rather pronounced.

After a few numbers *Epokha* went bankrupt, mainly on account of its unfortunate polemics with the radicals. In the same year Dostoevsky lost his wife and also his brother, whose widow and children now depended entirely upon him for support. He had been estranged from his wife for some time before joining her in Moscow towards the end of her illness. But when she died he wrote to Baron Wrangel that although their marriage had been unhappy, 'we could not stop loving one another. Indeed, the unhappier we were together, the stronger was our attachment.' It is quite possible that Dostoevsky was in love not so much with his wife, but with the torments which he had endured through her.

Soon after her death he was attracted (in the winter of 1864–5) by a certain Martha Brown—a destitute adventuress with an agitated and mysterious past. She was Russian, but nominally the wife of a Baltimore sailor. It was pity that played the main part in his interest in her. This cannot be said, however, of his affection for the vivacious young minx, Anna Korvin-Krukovskaya (the elder sister of the great woman-mathematician Sophie Kovalevskaya). His infatuation was serious enough; but when he proposed, Anna refused to marry him. Later he drew her portrait in Aglaya (*The Idiot*)—the most enchanting of his women characters.

As if anxious to increase the burdens that fell upon his shoulders after his brother's death, he made himself responsible for the liabilities of the defunct *Epokha*. His desperate financial situation may well be imagined. In spite of it, we find him in the summer of 1865 once more in Wiesbaden, where he was joined by Suslova. Once again he gambled desperately and lost all. Suslova hastily returned to Paris, leaving him at the mercy of penury or even starvation.

This is what he wrote, in his unstamped letter, to Suslova on August 22nd from Wiesbaden: 'As soon as you had left me, the very next day, I was told in the hotel that it was forbidden to give me lunch, tea or coffee. I demanded an explanation and the fat German proprietor said that I "deserved" no lunch, and that he would let me have only tea. So from yesterday tea has been my only food. And even the tea is extremely bad. . . . If you have reached Paris and if you can get something out of your friends and acquaintances, do send me a maximum of 150 guldens and a minimum of as much as you like. If I had 150 guldens I could be quits with these swine and change my hotel, while waiting for some money. . . .' And two days later: 'My affairs are bad beyond words; it would be impossible for them to be worse. One step farther, and I shall be in the welter of miseries and obscenities beyond imagination.'

At the most critical moment Dostoevsky is supposed to have been rescued by the priest of the local Russian church. Soon after he received 300 roubles from Katkov, the editor of *Russky Viestnik* (The Russian Messenger)— an advance on his prospective novel, *Crime and*

Punishment. Dostoevsky's four greatest novels were now destined to appear in Katkov's periodical.

Crime and Punishment (1866) firmly established his fame in Russia, and later in Western Europe. Financially, however, it failed to save him from his creditors or to bring some order into his existence. Several months earlier he had made, under the pressure of the notorious publisher Stellovsky, a contract either to deliver a whole novel before November 1st or else to forfeit all the financial benefit from his future writings. As the term was rapidly approaching, one of his friends (Milyukov) found a young stenographer, Anna Grigoryevna Snitkina, to whom Dostoevsky dictated his new work, *The Gambler*, with such speed as to finish it in time. This casual meeting between the author and the stenographer matured into love and a marriage which was totally different from Dostoevsky's experiences with his first wife. Anna Grigoryevna was an honest soul, very much *terre-à-terre*, practical, devoted and loyal: an ideal secretary and nurse in one. It is quite possible that on this occasion Dostoevsky married from prudence rather than passion, for he still continued—clandestinely—his correspondence with Suslova. Yet his wife's love and patience conquered him for the rest of his life. Unfortunately, his financial difficulties, added to by the greed of his relatives, now made such a confusion in his household, that he and his twenty-year-old wife preferred to take refuge in Western Europe.

This 'honeymoon' took them first to Germany. But in Baden-Baden Dostoevsky was again unable to resist the roulette table. All their money was gambled away, and he was forced to pawn his own and his wife's things. He lost and won, pawned and lost again, wrote desperate letters to Russia, and at last won a considerable sum which was lost yet again. Gambling like a maniac, first in Germany and later in Switzerland, he was unable to stop, though well aware of the utter misery that it threatened. His wife has described those trying weeks in a diary which was not published until 1923. Some of its pages seem all but incredible. One can hardly believe that a man who had passed through the ordeal of Siberian prisons could be so weak-willed and irresponsible. One is not surprised that even his wife's angelic patience failed her at last. Thus, on August 3rd, she wrote: 'O Lord, when shall we get out of this accursed mire in which we are stuck for good. I think we shall never get rid of it, but shall just continue to stick here gambling and gambling, hoping for a big win, until we are penniless.'

To make matters worse, it was in Baden that Dostoevsky's final breach with Turgenev took place—a breach which was only healed in the last year of Dostoevsky's life. Nevertheless, the first few months of this four-year vagabondage abroad released a new afflux of his creative energy, though they did nothing to ease the penury by which he was harassed. The chief item of Dostoevsky's letters to his friends and publishers at that time consists of urgent and humiliating requests for money. 'How can I work when I am hungry and have had to pawn even my pantaloons to get two thalers for the telegram,' he wrote to the poet A. Maikov on October 28th, 1869. 'The devil take me and hunger! But she, my wife, who is now suckling her infant, *she* had to go herself to the pawnshop and pledge her last warm woollen garments, and it has been snowing here for the last two days.'

One could quote even more desperate passages. If one adds to all this his extreme nervousness, his misunderstandings with lots of people, his growing aversion to the smug bourgeois spirit of Europe, his longing for Russia, the death of his child in Geneva, his inner doubts and torments, his attacks of epilepsy, one may obtain some idea of the conditions under which he wrote *The Idiot* (1868–9) and *The Possessed* (1871–2), both of which are among the profoundest novels in modern literature. His masterly short novel, *The Eternal Husband*, was also written abroad. Yet in spite of his physical ailments, such was the vitality of his spirit that he was able to surmount these hardships and even to participate in the general cultural activities of his homeland.

It should be borne in mind that those were the years of promise for Russia, the dawn of a new era as it were. After the liberation of the serfs by Tsar Alexander II, both Slavophils and Westerners spared no effort in their work for a better future. Dostoevsky himself had, of course, drawn nearer to the Slavophils: less for political than cultural reasons. This change is reflected in certain passages of *The Idiot*, and in the whole of *The Possessed* —a novel which may be regarded as his most vehement repudiation of the Western pseudo-progress and pseudo-civilization.

It was not civilization that Dostoevsky hated. Unlike Tolstoy, he loved it. But for that very reason he rejected its materialistic and soul-destroying trends so manifest to-day. While abroad he had seen enough of the West to fear its soulless capitalism, its noisy vulgarity and tedium. He could imagine no future worthy of mankind save by a complete reorganization, and was not Russia destined to lead the whole of mankind towards a better future? In the answer to this question Dostoevsky saw the very meaning of Russia's existence.

There came a time when this self-imposed exile began to weigh on him greatly. 'By God, without home life is torture!' he wrote to Maikov in 1867. 'I need Russia for my work, my life (I speak of no life than that). I am like a fish out of water; I lose all my energies, all my faculties. . . . I felt that so many new ideas had been garnered up, that I could write a long article about Russia's relation to Western Europe and the upper classes of Russian society. I should, indeed, have plenty to say! The Germans got on my nerves; and our Russian way of living, the life of the upper classes, the faith in Europe and civilization in which those upper classes are steeped —all that got on my nerves, too.'

What he missed was also that intimate human warmth which in a true Russian compensates for most of his defects. This is how he complains from Florence, in a letter to his niece (January 1869): 'In three months we shall have been exactly two years abroad. In my opinion it is worse than deportation to Siberia. I mean that quite seriously. I am not exaggerating. I cannot understand the Russians abroad. Even though there is a wonderful sky here, and though there are, as for example in Florence —literally unimaginable and incredible marvels of art, many advantages are lacking which even in Siberia, as soon as I left the prison, made themselves evident to me.' And later he confessed to his friend Maikov: 'If you knew what a deep-drawn repulsion, almost approaching hatred, I have conceived for the whole of Western Europe during those four years.'

In spite of such experiences, the problem of Russia and Europe expanded in Dostoevsky's mind until it included those ethical, social and religious aspects in which are steeped his novels and also his personal *Journal of an Author*—a miscellany which appeared in 1873, during 1867–8, and again shortly before his death.[1]

VI

Through his wife's energies Dostoevsky's material situation improved once he was back in Russia. Gradually he was able to settle his debts, to satisfy (more or less) even the greed of his relatives, and to enjoy during the last ten years of his life a certain amount of comfort. His fame was now undisputed. His influence was spreading. Hundreds of people were anxious to get his advice in difficulties of mind or conscience. His *Journal of an*

[1] In addition to a number of articles on all sorts of subjects, Dostoevsky published in it three of his most interesting stories: *A Gentle Spirit (Krotkaya), Bobok,* and *The Dream of a Queer Fellow.*

Author contained views and suggestions which were stimulating, even when they were not convincing. True enough, the voluminous novel, *A Raw Youth* (1875), which he wrote after his return to Russia, was somewhat disappointing if compared with such masterpieces as *Crime and Punishment* or *The Idiot*. But he made up for it in his last and greatest work, *The Brothers Karamazov* (printed in Katkov's *The Russian Messenger*, 1879–80).

After his long vagabondage, his malady and his mental crises, Dostoevsky was even now—at the age of sixty—full of vitality. This is how Melchior de Vogüe (who knew him personally during that period) describes him in his once famous *Le Roman Russe*: 'As a figure he resembles the chief scenes of his novels; whoever had seen it once could not forget it. How much it expressed his own work, his own life! Short, lean, utterly nervous, worn and weighted down by sixty years of misery, he seemed rather faded than aged. With his long beard and fair hair he had the look of an invalid of an uncertain age, and yet he was still emanating that "vitality of a cat" to which he once referred. His face was that of a Russian peasant—of a real moujik of Moscow, with an animated expression, now gloomy, now mild. His forehead was large, wrinkled and bumpy, his temples hollow as if beaten with a hammer; and all these drawn, convulsed features were drooping over a melancholy mouth. Never have I seen on a human face such an expression of accumulated suffering. All the crises of the soul and those of the body had left their mark on it. There one could read even more than in his books the memories from the *House of the Dead*, long periods of awe, of doubt and of martyrdom. His eyelids, his lips, each muscle of his face, twitched with nervous spasms. Whenever he became excited or angry in disputes over ideas, one could have sworn that one had seen that face before—either on the benches of the criminal court or among those vagabonds whose road leads to the prison gates. At all other moments his face was full of that sad meekness which is characteristic of the old saints painted on the Slavonic ikons. Everything in this man was of the people, with the inexpressible mixture of coarseness, subtlety and sweetness which the Russian peasants so often possess; and a something indefinably troubling, resulting perhaps from the expression of concentrated thought on that mask of a proletarian. At first he often repelled—before his strange personal magnetism began to have effect.'

As though beguiled by his own 'vitality of a cat', Dostoevsky died sooner than had been expected by those who knew him. On June 8th, 1880, he delivered, during the Pushkin celebrations, his speech on the greatest Russian poet. The speech turned into an unheard-of personal triumph for Dostoevsky himself. It was the culmination of his literary and public activities. A few months later he was preparing to continue *The Journal of an Author* when all his plans were cut short by his sudden death on January 28th, 1881.

II

DOSTOEVSKY AS ARTIST

I

IF we consider works of art and literature from the angle of their genesis, we notice several, often contradictory impulses of creation. One of them is the author's need to find a refuge from the burden of actual life either in an imaginary world or in wishful thinking. Another is the secret craving to take revenge upon life for one's frustrations, especially for one's disappointed idealism. In this case satirical mockery and sneering realism are likely to come into their own. At the opposite end is the impulse to play with reality in the benevolently humorous mood, known only to a man whose sense of proportion is strong enough to prevent him from taking too seriously either himself or the world—a disposition which makes him smile where a wounded idealist would grin, or gnash his teeth. Then there is the urge to enlarge one's perception of reality through exploring its wider aspects, its secrets, beauties, and also its horrors. In so far as this urge is expressed through the medium of literature, we obtain various grades of realism.

An artist who is on the look-out for an escape is usually drawn towards 'romance'. He indulges in imaginary substitutes for an intense life and clings to them all the more tenaciously the more he is repelled by the actual world. Exotic romanticism and hot-house aestheticism are often but shelters, prompted by one's inability to accept life, or to grapple with its difficulties. A true realist, on the other hand, enjoys above all the manifold variety of existence. In contrast to a romantic, he feels at home in this world even when he rebels against its negative aspects. His art gives us an intensified picture of life as seen through his creative eye. Yet this picture is never entirely 'detached'. It is bound to be more or less subjective for the very reason that the world it presents is sifted through his personal vision and temperament.

Such impulses need not function singly. Some of them pass into each other, intertwining in a startling manner. Thus a romantic 'escapist' whose imagination is too weak to provide an adequate shelter, often goes back to real life, but with an aggressive and rancorous attitude. What he wants is to take revenge upon life. He watches it, preys upon it, all the time anxious to show up its squalor and meanness. In this process he uses realistic methods, but the impulse behind it all is romantic. What he is after is the refutation of life as it is. Yet he often enjoys —sometimes ecstatically so—his own *Weltschmerz*. His romantic disgust can in fact give him a feeling of superiority over the life he criticizes, as well as over ordinary mortals and their doings. European realism is full of disguised romantics. Flaubert is one of them. So is Gogol. So is Thomas Hardy.

A more complicated realist is the man who for some reason or other accepts life as an artist, even if his moral or social sense takes up a highly negative attitude. An example of a full-blooded biological acceptance of life in the teeth of one's protesting moral sense is Tolstoy. Tolstoy's work as a whole shows a tragic contest between the two attitudes—a contest which eventually turned that great artist into a moral preacher. Finally, an organizing artistic vision of the world may be combined with a strong sociological interest, as was the case with Balzac—one of the creators of the modern novel. These two elements are often at variance. And when a didactic vein is added to it, journalism, popular science, and social propaganda are smuggled into literature. There are several degrees of such art (which can be quite stimulating at times) from Zola to H. G. Wells, from Brieux and Shaw to the enthusiastic Soviet authors. The question that remains open is in how far they are aesthetically satisfactory.

A very intensive kind of realism can be obtained however by concentrating on man's inner world. It results in the psychological novel pure and simple, or else in that type of novel in which a religious-philosophic quest merges with 'psychology' to such an extent as to become one with it. A quest of this kind frequently represents the author's own inner travail—exteriorized and projected into human characters whose 'philosophy' is not a matter of intellect only, but of what might be called one's total inner experience.

Ideas which had been lived, i.e. tested through one's entire consciousness and then embodied in living characters, were the mainspring of Dostoevsky's novels.

II

A conventional approach to Dostoevsky would be out of place, since he himself is one of the least conventional authors. This does not mean, however, that he developed apart from or outside the influences and traditions then prevalent. Hoffmann, Balzac, Eugène Sue, George Sand and others have already been mentioned. As for his Russian predecessors, he himself acknowledged his indebtedness to Gogol. His agitated style (so different from the quiet 'Apollonian' manner, bequeathed by Pushkin to Turgenev, Goncharov and Tolstoy) goes chiefly back to Gogol, and perhaps also to the French humanitarian romantics of the 'thirties. The 'natural school', as represented by Gogol and preached by Belinsky, was responsible for his interest in the 'insulted and injured', even if the downtrodden copying clerk had become a worn-out theme by the time Dostoevsky took him up—sentimentally in *Poor Folk*, and grotesquely in *The Double*.

Dostoevsky's love of involved mysterious plots was another feature which connected him with romanticism. So was his love of extreme antitheses and particularly his interest in the irrational which he combined, however, with an uncanny psychological sense. Prying into the most hidden recesses of man's soul and spirit, he was the first European novelist to explore the unconscious and to annex it wholesale to modern literature. Yet he was too much of a brooding analyst to be a reliable observer of externals. Nor did he care for the traditional homogeneity of character, since he was only too familiar with the contrasts and contradictions of the human ego. What attracted him above all was that inner chaos which compels one to look for some outlet from among the greatest antinomies. In such an effort 'psychology' and spiritual quest converge as a rule, yet the result of their union is something utterly different from the abstract arm-chair philosophy. Here ideas are tested through living experience, through one's entire personality. They become dynamic 'ideas-emotions' (to use a word coined by Dostoevsky himself), or perhaps ideas-forces. If these assume a predominantly philosophic expression, something like *Thus Spake Zarathustra*, Pascals's *Pensées*, or Kierkegaard's writings may result. If, however, creative imagination and plastic vision be their vehicle, then Dostoevsky's novels or their equivalents become possible.

Dostoevsky usually starts with some vital inner problem which determines the trend of his intuitions, observations and ideas. But instead of pasting the ideas upon his characters, he makes them an organic part of their inner make-up, no matter whether he himself agrees with what they say or not. Moreover, during the creative process his leading idea itself becomes split into its own conflicting antitheses which open up dramatic possibilities of a new kind. The very form of a Dostoevskian novel results from the dynamic tension between several contradictory planes and trends of one and the same consciousness—each of them with its own conclusions.

The principle of fugue, of 'symphonic' treatment, is possible in a novel only if the author gives the most opposite themes and motives an equal chance. And this is what Dostoevsky does. His favourite methods are those in which not only the inner life, but also the personal tone of the characters described comes out to the best advantage in the relationship to their own opposites. This is why a number of his works are written in the first person (*Notes from the Underworld*, *The Gambler*, *The Insulted and Injured*, *The Possessed*, *A Raw Youth*, etc.). He was also a past master at rendering the split inner dialogue: in *The Double*, and especially in Ivan Karamazov. Another favourite method of his to achieve a maximum of personal accent is that of confession, so frequently interpolated in his novels: Ippolit's confession in *The Idiot*, for example, Stavrogin's in *The Possessed* (later deleted), or of the elder Zosima in *The Brothers Karamazov*. His important *Notes from the Underworld* preserves the accent of a confession from the first to the last line.

Dostoevsky confronts dramatically not only antinomic characters, but antinomic features in one and the same character. In doing this, he preserves complete spiritual and intellectual fairness, no matter how acute or how personal his own attitude may be. Entire chapters of his have a power of their own precisely because they are so ambiguous. The finale of *Crime and Punishment*, or of 'The Legend of the Grand Inquisitor' in *The Brothers Karamazov* would be less powerful if it were less inconclusive.

Only an author capable of projecting his own inner chaos and travail into living characters, in order to achieve a kind of *katharsis*, could have written as Dostoevsky did. For him art was a relentless urge, perhaps an alternative to madness. This explains why some of his creations are so intense as to haunt the reader's imagination like spooks. Sometimes they affect one as nightmares and symbols in one—even symbols of forces which seem to transcend our ordinary plane of existence. It is at this point that

Dostoevsky's 'realism' asserts itself in a peculiar and original fashion.

III

We may perhaps find a clue to his realism by drawing a line between reality and actuality. The two are often regarded as identical. Yet reality is more than actuality. It includes all the hidden forces and agents of life, whereas actuality is confined to its external or else 'topical' aspects. The proportion between these two planes varies and is reflected in the two different although complementary directions in art, especially in the novel: the horizontal and the vertical.

The 'horizontal' novel is concerned with manners, with life as expressed in terms of external contacts and relationships of the persons described. But it must not stop here. Unless it has a fringe, suggestive of something more important and universal than what it shows, it will remain only a picture or document of a certain period— nearer to journalism than to art. The 'vertical' novel, however, concentrates above all upon human destinies as they work in and through the characters presented. Hence it is predominantly psychological. It is more intensive than extensive; for which purpose it reduces the number of characters, as well as the area of their background, to a minimum. If the 'horizontal' novel is analogous to the old epic on the one hand and to comedy on the other, the 'vertical' novel finds its counterpart in the drama. And as for social manners, it is interested in them in so far as they can be a matter of conflict with the individual who turns against tradition in the name of his own vision of life, or of his own inner freedom. The entire problem of evil, for example, with its ultimate metaphysical implications, is dealt with by Dostoevsky only on this plane. And so intensely, too, that some of his characters may even strike one as agents of cosmic forces of good and evil.

He thus enlarged and deepened the scope of the European novel. He added to it a new dimension as it were. Some of the early European modernists were quick enough to see this. K. J. Huysmanns, for instance, wrote in his *Là-bas*: 'The main path, so deeply worn by Zola, would have to be followed; but at the same time a parallel track ought to be pursued in the air, in order to explore the things of the hidden beyond—in a word, to produce a spiritual naturalism. The man who can be mentioned in particular as having approached this conception is Dostoevsky.' 'Spiritual realism' is the label applied to Dostoevsky's art by Melchior de Voguë, in his pioneering work on the Russian novel. And Dostoevsky himself is quite explicit about it when he says in one of his letters: 'I have a totally different conception of truth and realism from that of our "realists" and critics. My God! If one could tell but categorically all that we Russians have gone through during the last ten years in the way of spiritual development, all the realists would shriek that it was pure fantasy! And yet it would be pure realism! It is the one true, deep realism. Theirs is altogether too superficial.' And again, 'I have my own ideas about art, and it is this: what most people regard as fantastic and lacking in universality, I hold to be the inmost essence of truth. Arid observations of everyday trivialities I have long ceased to regard as realism—it is quite the reverse. . . . I am a realist in the higher meaning of the term.'

If a label were necessary at all, we could perhaps call his art *visionary* realism, as distinct from mere visual realism. He strains the actual and the average to its utmost limits mainly in order to reach that reality which lies beyond it. His wildest and cruellest situations are often but experiments upon the human soul with the object of extracting its 'inmost essence'. Hence there is something paradoxical about Dostoevsky's exaggerated characters: they are most real when they seem least realistic from the standpoint of the mere visual realism.

IV

Dostoevsky's work (like that of any great author) can best be understood if regarded in the perspective of his general perception and intuition of life. Yet in his case we must take into consideration the three planes which he usually intermingles. The first is the plane of *byt*[1] or the social background. The second is the purely psychological plane. And the third—the most important among them—is the one in which 'psychology' passes into the sphere of spiritual experience and valuations.

The first of these three planes matters in so far as it expresses a complete absence of fixed or stable social forms. In Dostoevsky's writings everything is in a 'flux', including the social classes which are chaotically mixed up. His principal heroes are taken, as it were, out of all social causality—a fact which gives the author an even greater freedom in dwelling upon the fundamentals of human life, upon the tragic conflicts of mind and spirit. Yet while stripping his characters of external bonds and conventions, Dostoevsky adopted a number of external devices to keep the attention of his readers. A study of his technique may reveal tricks which resemble those of the sensational 'lower' fiction: the criminal or detective novel, the melodramatic newspaper serial, and even the penny shocker. In his novel, *The Insulted and Injured*, for example, we see an aristocratic weakling in love with a poor girl who is victimized by a diabolically 'clever' prince. Cursed by her father, the girl passes from one humiliation to the other, until she dies. There is in it also the hackneyed theme of the lost child who, after all sorts of ordeals, proves to be of exalted birth, etc. Only Dostoevsky could permit himself such cheap tricks and yet create great novels. He often adjusted his external plots to the level of the average reader; but at

[1] An untranslatable Russian word which means the manners together with the entire social atmosphere of a class or a period.

the same time he made them only scaffoldings for what lay beyond them. Thus the 'thrilling' detective element in *Crime and Punishment* is almost irrelevant as compared with the principal 'idea-force' of the novel: the idea of moral self-will.

Another reason why Dostoevsky loved to pile up so many unusual plots and events was his tendency to experiment with the human self: to put it into the most incredible situations, and watch its reactions. He was drawn towards such plots as would enable him to study the farthest limits of consciousness. Yet however complicated his plots may be, they develop with and through the characters. The motives of action thus remain internal. And once these motives have reached the intensity suggestive of supra-human agencies (whether of good or evil), Dostoevsky magnifies his characters accordingly; or at least his male characters, because his women are never treated on the same spiritual scale as his men. Nor must we forget the discrepancy between the external, astronomical, and the inner, psychic time which is so conspicuous in some of his works. Many of his heroes seem to have lived inwardly through centuries, whereas the simultaneous external events have lasted a few hours only, perhaps a few days. This new sense of time, resembling the accelerated time-experience in our dreams, is the exact reverse of the recent experiments by another psychologist: Marcel Proust. Instead of accelerating, Proust has slowed the time down—in the way certain films are done in order to show the minutest details of the subject in motion.

Dostoevsky had so much to say that the forms of the old novel proved inadequate. He had to work out a 'symphonic' form of his own whose style is often jerky, and composition uneven. As he himself said in a letter to Strakhov: 'With me several novels are condensed into one which, for this very reason, lacks harmony and balance.' Most satisfactory, formally, are some of his smaller novels, such as *The Gambler* and *The Eternal Husband*, written at one sitting as it were. Among the big novels *Crime and Punishment* is best in construction, although the crime itself takes place before the motivation of the crime is given. The action begins right in the middle and then is gradually unravelled in concentric circles—from the periphery towards the focus. *The Idiot*, too, is carried out well. Less satisfactory is *The Possessed*, in which the gruesome subject-matter is not sufficiently sublimated by art. Here, if anywhere, one often feels the truth of Mme Dostoevsky's statement (in her *Memoirs*) that during the whole of his life there was not a single work, except *Poor Folk*, her husband had not written in a hurry. The same applies even in greater measure to *A Raw Youth*. However interesting its theme, we do not feel in it the same balance between art, psychology, and dynamic ideas as we do in *Crime and Punishment*.

Such a balance is, however, evident again in *The Brothers Karamazov*, Dostoevsky's last and longest novel. Each part of this monumental work is almost a novel in itself, yet they all converge towards the denouement in the finale. The contrast between the brothers is worked out with unsurpassed subtlety. Moreover, while reading this masterpiece, we actually follow its parallel development on the three mentioned planes. We watch the background of a Russian town, the involved psychological experiences of the main characters, and the spiritual import of it all. One of its great features is the delightful gallery of boys, each of them depicted with consummate understanding of a child's mind. In addition, Ivan Karamazov's 'Legend of the Grand Inquisitor' gives us the most dramatic philosophy of history ever presented in literary form.

v

The influence of Dostoevsky on modern world literature has been enormous, greater than that of Tolstoy. Among his partial followers are such widely different authors as

Nietzsche and Bourget, Hauptmann and d'Annunzio, André Gide and the German expressionists. In England the interest in his work has been rather fluctuating and confined mainly to the highbrows. *The House of the Dead* was his first book to appear in English, in 1881. It was followed, five years later, by *Crime and Punishment*. He came into fashion only after 1910, especially in the early 'twenties, during the vogue of psycho-analysis.

During those years the English novel, too, began to show signs of his influence. Joseph Conrad, who combined so ingeniously the old picaresque novel with an impressionist technique and the up-to-date psychological subtleties, never made a secret of his dislike of Dostoevsky. Yet he must have read him carefully, for *Under Western Eyes* is unmistakably (although unsuccessfully) 'Dostoevskian'. Quite a strong influence of Dostoevsky is noticeable in Hugh Walpole's early works: in *The Dark Forest*, for example, or in his Petrograd novel, *The Secret City*, where a character—the doctor—is a copy of Svidrigailov (*Crime and Punishment*). D. H. Lawrence fumed at the great Russian, but in his cult of the irrational he was nearer to him than any other English author. There are quite a few traces of Dostoevsky's influence in some other modernists—even if the English novel has too strong a tradition of its own to take him as seriously as he was taken in Central Europe, for instance.

In Russia Dostoevsky affected the modern novel through such talented followers as Andrei Bely, and (in Soviet literature) Leonid Leonov. But as neither his Russian nor Western-European emulators could produce writers of his calibre, his many-sided heritage became split along several channels. Some of his followers seized upon the clinical aspects of his work, making use of them for a new species of sensational literature. Others adopted Dostoevsky's tragic antinomies, but as these did not come from their inmost experience, the usual result was that pseudo-tragic pose to which Leonid Andreyev, for example, sacrificed all that was genuine in him. A third group succumbed to the shibboleths of the 'naked soul' and the 'romanticism of the nerves' (like the Polish decadent Stanislaw Przybyszewski), not to mention several other 'isms'.

As for Dostoevsky's religious, social, and philosophic ideas, these proved a great challenge to the Russian generation of the 'sixties and the 'seventies. In the 'eighties the interest in his work diminished, but came into its own once more at the beginning of this century. Merezhkovsky's famous study, *Tolstoy and Dostoevsky* (1901–3), can be considered a landmark in the Dostoevsky cult among the pre-war Russian intellectuals. So can V. Rozanov's *The Legend of the Grand Inquisitor* (1902). Joined by the belated influence of the philosopher Vladimir Solovyev, this cult was largely responsible for the formation of the neo-idealist group of Russian philosophy which is still active. Some of its members— Bulgakov and Nikolai Berdyaev—enjoy an international reputation. The current, represented by this group, has strongly affected the character of the Russian symbolism as represented by Andrei Bely, Vyacheslav Ivanov, and Alexander Blok.

Dostoevsky's influence will continue to fluctuate. Yet quite independently of literary fashions, he will always appeal to those who are drawn towards the deeper aspects of life and the human mind.

III

DOSTOEVSKY AS PSYCHOLOGIST

I

THE work of any great author is conditioned—apart from his talent—by his personality on the one hand, and by the age in which he lives on the other. The proportion between the two varies. So does the immediate effect of his writings. The deeper and more complicated his personality, the more is he likely to strike his own contemporaries as something puzzling or even disturbing, especially when he defies the conventional notions of his epoch. Hence the jungle of contradictory judgments, passed on Dostoevsky. The bitterest of them all is perhaps the one expressed by the critic Strakhov in a letter he wrote to Tolstoy soon after Dostoevsky's death. 'I cannot consider Dostoevsky either a good or a happy man,' he says. 'He was wicked, envious, vicious, and he spent the whole of his life in emotions and irritations which would have made him pitiable, even ridiculous, had he not been so wicked and so intelligent. . . . In Switzerland he treated his servant, in my presence, so abominably that the latter cried out, offended: "I too am a human being." . . . Naturally, he more often offended people in order not to be offended by them, but the most terrible thing about it was that he enjoyed it and never acknowledged his villainies to the end.'

Even if we refuse to take Strakhov's incriminations at their face value, the 'underworld' element remained strong enough in Dostoevsky to make Turgenev once label him 'the most evil Christian I have ever met in my life'. Yet whatever his faults, Dostoevsky was always able to redeem them by the opposite qualities. His daughter Lyubov (Aimée) even contends, in an unreliable biography, that her father was something of an immaculate bourgeois after the Western pattern. And his second wife, Anna Grigoryevna, says in her *Memoirs* that the fourteen years of her married life had convinced her that Dostoevsky was the purest being on earth.

No less contradictory are the attitudes towards Dostoevsky the author. Sincerely enthusiastic are the studies by Suarès, Gide, and Middleton Mury. D. H. Lawrence, on the other hand, exclaims (in his preface to a new English translation of *The Grand Inquisitor*): 'As always in Dostoevsky, the amazing perspicacity is mixed up with ugly perversity. Nothing is pure. Dostoevsky is always perverse, always impure, always an evil thinker and a marvellous seer.' Negative, with a dash of smug superficiality, is the attitude of George Moore.

Last but not least, the founder of modern psychoanalysis, Sigmund Freud, endeavours to explain (in his essay, *Dostoevsky and Parricide*) some of Dostoevsky's features by means of the 'Oedipus complex'. While dissecting his feeling of guilt and his urge towards self-abasement, suffering, and expiation, Freud argues that Dostoevsky the boy must have had a strong desire to murder his hateful father—a desire which he soon identified with the crime itself. When his father had actually been murdered by his own serfs, this subconscious disposition was followed by a strong feeling of guilt and by a craving for punishment. He enjoyed piling upon himself voluntary suffering, misfortunes, and humiliations. In fact, these gave him a moral relief, and even stimulated his creative power. Dostoevsky's strong instinct of destruction—an instinct which might have led him to crime—was thus practised above all against himself. Having turned within and not without, it assumed the shape of masochism. 'Dostoevsky was in small matters a sadist whose sadism was practised upon himself; that is, he was a masochist, and consequently the tenderest, the best and the most obliging human being.'

This diagnosis, so different from that of Strakhov, is much too clinical. It misses the paradoxical fact that Dostoevsky probably *needed* not only his feeling of guilt, but even actual moral lapses—in order to feed upon them spiritually. He was a man whose loftiest moods and emotions could best be evoked by their own contrasts. But even apart from that, a sin may not always be a spiritual evil, since the moral and the spiritual planes need not necessarily coincide. Experience through sin and suffering often fosters one's inner growth and enriches one's spirit infinitely more than a static and carefully protected virtue could ever do. Even in some of its dangerous aspects it is less of a blight than the complacent puritanism which kills one's spirit and narrows one down to a self-righteous moral smug. A person aware of his own imperfections, and suffering from them, is always likely to develop that tolerance and generosity which comes from a true understanding of human nature, of human weakness. And this itself is a rare virtue.

II

Dostoevsky was certainly endowed with such understanding. Besides, what he was after was not morality, but the intensity and fullness of life. And such fullness may demand also negative experiences, unhappiness, as well as that intense struggle with one's inner contradictions through which alone perhaps one's spirit can mature. The problem of good and evil which crops up on the plane of the spirit is something much more formidable than the sterile moral book-keeping of the puritans. And it was on this plane only that Dostoevsky tackled it. Even his interest in psychology was largely dictated by implications which go beyond mere psychology.

What Dostoevsky wanted to find out, was the working of the human spirit in and through man's consciousness. And the more involved this working the more it attracted him. That was why he was preoccupied with the three main paths, leading one to the greatest tension of consciousness: the mystical experience, the crime, and the suffering. He purposely neglected average happenings and the average normal man. It was only the deviations from the normal that appealed to him. In these he sought for the secret of the normal itself. His explorations of the diseased mental states were not of a clinical kind. They were only a short-cut to that 'inmost essence' of man and life which average healthy conditions could not provide. Thus the epileptic prince Myshkin (*The Idiot*) used to pass, before his fits, through moments of inner harmony which a normal person would hardly understand.

'These moments,' Myshkin reasoned, 'short as they are, when I feel such extreme consciousness of myself, and consequently more life than at other times, are due only to disease—to the sudden rupture of normal conditions. . . . What matter though it be only disease, an abnormal tension of the brain, if when I recall and analyse that moment, it seems to have been one of harmony and beauty in the highest degree—an instant of deepest sensation, overflowing with unbounded joy and rapture, ecstatic devotion, and completest life.'

Such, on the whole, was Dostoevsky's own attitude.[1] He knew from personal experience that what at the first glance looks sick and pathologic, may easily stir up human consciousness to activities which are supra-normal rather than abnormal. These two aspects may appear equally diseased on the surface, yet one of them leads to degenerate regression, while the other often marks the birth-pangs of a new consciousness, of a 'higher health'. Thanks only to the confusion of the abnormal and the supra-normal, was it possible to class (as Lombroso did) the genius with the insane and the criminal, and to accept

[1] As Ernest J. Simmons points out in his *Dostoevsky*, a number of his deductions were anticipated by C. G. Carus, whose *Psyche* (1846) Dostoevsky intended to translate, when he was in Semipalatinsk.

as an ideal the average normal type with his robust nervous system and his limited psyche. A rich, highly differentiated inner life is often both painful and 'morbid' —especially in an age which has undermined all certainty, all stability. And the richer one's inner life, the more it is likely to set up intellect against intuition, the 'normal' against the 'abnormal', the unconscious against the conscious, until one's ego is threatened by a process of utter self-division.

Most of Dostoevsky's pyschology was a struggle against such a process—a struggle in which he was compelled to explore the inner world in all directions simply in order to find an outlet for himself. His favourite ground was, however, that fluctuating area where the rational passes into the irrational, the conscious into the unconscious, the actual into the 'fantastic'. He was a supreme connoisseur of that region of the soul where nothing is fixed and firm; where 'all contradictions exist side by side'. It was here that he made some of his strangest discoveries. These he turned into creative art: creative in the sense of both literature and life.

III

Dostoevsky the psychologist had fully anticipated our present interest in the Unconscious. Long before Freud, he saw in dreams symbolic projections of our unconscious self—without reducing them, however, to a mere sexual *libido*. The dreams of Raskolinov, the nightmare of Ippolit in *The Idiot*, or of Ivan Karamazov have nothing to do with sex. True enough, we find in Dostoevsky's works all forms of erotic passion: from the awakening of innocent love to the perversions of Svidrigailov, Stavrogin, and the old Karamazov. Yet unlike Freud, he saw man's basic urge not in sex, but in the will to assert and to affirm his own ego; in the 'will to power'.

Even in *Poor Folk* we see how the humble scribe tries to stand on his dignity and to assert himself in his own modest way. Golyadkin, the hero of *The Double*, is so anxious to forget his social nothingness that his unconscious projects outside himself an antipodes of his actual ego and makes him live an independent life of his own. Foma Opiskin (in *The Village Stepanchikovo*), formerly a despised and crushed individual, becomes a despot as soon as he feels power in his hands. He wants to humiliate every one he can in order to increase the illusion of his own power and significance. More complicated is the self-assertion in *Notes from the Underworld*. Its hero is all the time concerned with other people's opinions about him. But as he knows that their opinions are low, he reacts by rancour and scorn which feed on his secret wish to be understood, respected, and loved. In this work the analysis of self-assertion on a purely psychological plane reached a limit after which the author was bound to tackle those new regions which point from mere self-assertion to self-realization in the name of higher over-personal values.

In his definition of self-assertiveness Dostoevsky came close to various aspects of Nietzsche's 'will to power', and also of the *ego libido*, connected with the theories of Alfred Adler. In his *Theory of Individual Psychology* Adler even maintains that 'any one who has felt to what degree Dostoevsky has recognised the *tendency to despotism* implanted in the human soul, will admit that Dostoevsky must be regarded as our teacher even to-day, as the teacher Nietzsche hailed him to be. His understanding and his discussion of the dream have not been superseded even to-day, and his idea that no one acts or thinks without a goal or a final climax, coincides with the most modern results of students of the psyche.'

This 'tendency to despotism' may of course be prompted also by the sex *libido* in which Dostoevsky was keenly interested, knowing however full well that the latter was only one of the channels. The erotic symbolism of a number of dreams in his novels (especially Svidrigailov's dream before his suicide) is matchless. So is the manner in which he unfolds the 'Oedipus complex' in *The Brothers Karamazov*. The rivalry between Mitya and his father, the hatred between the old Karamazov and his sons, Ivan's loathing for his half-brother Mitya, and the subconscious tricks by which he gets rid of him as well as of his father—all this is superbly motivated and described. But since Dostoevsky himself was drawn towards the problem of 'power' in the *metaphysical* sense, he gradually concentrated on the psychology of self-assertion in its deeper implications.

It was for this reason that he first attacked our old ideas of happiness. He contended that what man is after is not 'rational' happiness, but the intensity of life he obtains from the affirmation of his will and of his own ego, even if he had to distort the whole of life for such a purpose. Dostoevsky further demonstrated that when this ego cannot be asserted except through suffering, destruction, and even self-destruction, the *homo sapiens* will madly plunge into them in spite of all the theories preached by Mill and other utilitarian positivists. This is how his 'man from the Underworld' reasons on the subject:

'Who was it first said that man does evil because he is blind to his own interests, but that if he were enlightened, if his eyes were opened to his real, his normal interests, he would at once cease to do evil, and become virtuous and noble for the reason that, being now enlightened and brought to understand what is best for him, he would discern his true advantage only in what is good (since it is a known thing that no man of set purpose acts against his own interest), and therefore would of necessity also *do* what is good? Oh, the utter artlessness of the prattlers! . . . Does not reason err in estimating what is advantageous? May it not be that man occasionally loves something besides prosperity? May it not be that he loves *adversity*? Certainly there are times when man *does* love adversity, and love it passionately.

Man is a frivolous creature, and, like a chess-player, cares more for the process of attaining his goal than for the goal itself. Besides, who know (for it never does to be sure) that the aims which man strives for upon earth may not be contained in this ceaseless continuation of the process of the attainment—that is to say, in the process which is comprised in the living of life rather than in the aim itself, which, of course, is contained in the formula that twice two make four? Yet, gentlemen, this formula is not life at all; it is only the beginning of death! At all events, men have always been afraid to think that twice two make four, and I am afraid of it, too!'

After a few sarcasms about the compulsory Millennium to come (built on logic, reason, and statistics), he concludes: 'I should not be surprised if amidst all this order and regularity of the future, there should arise suddenly, from some quarter or another, some gentleman of low-born—or, rather, of retrograde and cynical demeanour, who, setting his arms akimbo, should say to you all: "How now, gentlemen? Would it not be a good thing if, with one consent, we were to kick all this solemn wisdom to the winds, to send those logarithms to the devil, and to begin to live our lives again according to our own stupid whims?" Yet this would be nothing: the really shameful part of the business would be that this gentleman would find a goodly number of adherents. Such is always man's way. . . . Whence do savants have it that man needs a normal, a virtuous will? What, in particular, has made these pundits imagine that what man most needs is a will which is acutely alive to man's interests? Why, what man most needs is an *independent* will—no matter what the cost of such independence of volition, nor what it may lead to!'

IV

The most striking of Dostoevsky's discoveries in the psychology of self-assertion are, however, the ones referring to the 'insulted and injured'; to persons suffering from irreparable injustice on the one hand, and from an acute feeling of their own inferiority on the other. Again and again he took up the weakling who has been insulted without being able to retaliate, and therefore turns all his rancour against himself, humiliating himself even more, as if revelling in his own degradation. 'Strange to say,' reasons Arkady in *A Raw Youth*, 'I always had, perhaps from my earliest childhood, one characteristic: if I were ill-treated, absolutely wronged and insulted to the last degree, I always showed at once an irresistible desire to submit passively to the insult, and even to accept more than my assailant wanted to inflict on me, as though I would say: "All right, you have humiliated me, so I will humiliate myself even more; look, and enjoy it." ' Such voluntary self-degradation can in fact give one the illusion of what might be called self-will from the other end: one is utterly humiliated at least through one's *own* (and not other people's) volition.

An aggressive counterpart of it is the sadistic self-assertion of a weakling who wants to bully and tyrannize over every one he can get hold of. It is a known fact that erotic sadists often suffer from sexual inferiority or even impotence. Similarly, mental and moral cruelty is to be found above all in people who are not sure either of their own value or of their own convictions. The Holy Inquisition was not a child of faith, but of incipient doubt. And the cruellest inquisitors were probably those who feared their own latent unbelief. According to Dostoevsky (*Crime and Punishment*) even murder can arise from the urge to prove and to assert one's 'will to power' over another human being in an absolute way, i.e. by taking his life.

Exaggerated moral cruelty finds, however, its masochist contrast in that exaggerated pity which was another favourite motive of Dostoevsky the psychologist. But through certain kinds of pity one can affirm oneself against the person one pities nearly as much as one does through cruelty. Pity is often but cruelty turned inside out, and—in contrast to love—is equally devoid of respect. The dividing line between the two is much narrower than is generally thought. Did not Dostoevsky often invent the greatest torments for his characters that he might shed tears of pity over them? And as for certain motives of charity, he made this remark (in his drafts for *The Life of a Great Sinner*) about one of his heroes: 'Out of pride and infinite haughtiness towards people he becomes meek and charitable to all, because he is already higher than all.' Such meekness is perhaps the subtlest form of *indirect* self-assertion; a form of pride which Nietzsche overlooked in his sweeping dissection of 'Christian' mentality.[1]

Another feature of Dostoevsky's explorations was his constant emphasis on the Unconscious. The value of his intuitions in this respect has been endorsed by so many authorities that it hardly requires any further eulogies. His novels and stories teem with passages which might be taken as illustrations even for the most up-to-date text-books. In addition, he is always close to the line where psychology passes into 'metapsychology'. Ivan's nightmare talk with the devil is an example. Another instance is Stavrogin's talk with Father Tikhon in the monastery, as recorded in the deleted *Stavrogin's Confession*. Stavrogin, like Ivan Karamazov, suffers from hallucinations in which he sees the devil. But while telling the monk about it, he adds:

'This is all nonsense, utter nonsense. It is myself in various aspects, and nothing else. But even as I use that phrase, you certainly think that I am still doubtful and am not really believing in the devil.'

Tikhon gave him a questioning look.

'And you actually see him?' he asked, dismissing, in

---

[1] A remarkable instance of charity and meekness from pride is Tolstoy's *Father Sergius*.

fact, any question of its being a false and morbid hallu-
cination. 'Do you actually see a certain image?'

'It is strange that you should lay stress upon this, when
I have already told you that I do see it.' Stavrogin again
began to grow more and more agitated with each word.
'Of course I see it; I see it as plainly as I see you . . .
and sometimes I see it and I'm not sure that I see it,
although I do see it . . . and sometimes I do not know
what is real: I or it . . . it's all nonsense. And can't you
possibly believe that this is indeed the devil?' he added,
breaking into a laugh and passing too abruptly into
cynicism: 'Surely that would be more in keeping with
your profession.'

One finds in Dostoevsky a number of similar 'border-
line' cases, connected, as a rule, with his main psychological problem: the problem of the 'double', of the
multiple personality. No modern novelist has treated the
latter with such clairvoyance and in so many aspects as
Dostoevsky. Practically each of his important characters
suffers from self-division and is therefore in the grip of
continuous inner antinomies, or of a strange hide-and-seek
game with others, as well as with himself. Not only their
ideas, but their very words, too, often become split and as
though disintegrating. Hence the 'diverging' dialogue of
so many of his characters. There is a difference between
what they say and what they mean; or even what they
would like to mean.

v

Golyadkin, the hero of *The Double*, was Dostoevsky's
first multiple personality, suffering from an irresistible
urge towards self-assertion. And the skill with which the
author turned that case of 'schizophrenia' into a literary
masterpiece is amazing. Golyadkin's ordinary self is quite
rational, law-abiding, and zealous in the discharge of
civic and private duties. His subconscious *alter ego* (projected outside himself in the person of a fellow clerk), is,

however, the opposite of all that: impudent and more than ready to push himself forward by the foulest tricks—at the expense of the first Golyadkin. The submissive first Golyadkin tries to make friends with the 'other Golyadkin', but in vain: his double's kiss is a kiss of Judas. Unable to overcome his own self-division, he goes mad.

This tragi-comic *déclassé* is the prototype of all self-divided characters in Dostoevsky's later and greater novels. Theirs is Golyadkin's fate, but amplified and shown in a spiritual perspective. Like Golyadkin, they have their 'doubles' who rise out of their unconscious and invade their will, their logic and reason. The individual now sides with one then with the other self, or with both simultaneously, thus accommodating in his ego the most painful contrasts.

'I am really split in two mentally, and am horribly afraid of it,' Versilov complains in *A Raw Youth*. 'It is just as though one's *second self* were standing beside one: one is sensible and rational oneself, but the other is impelled to do something perfectly senseless and very funny: and suddenly you notice you are longing to do that amusing thing, goodness knows why. I once knew a doctor who suddenly began whistling in the church, at his father's funeral.'

'The more I have recognized what is good and what constitutes "the great and the beautiful", the deeper I have plunged into the mire and the more I have been ready to smear myself with the sticky stuff. The most curious point of all is this—that the mood which I have described never seemed to be a mere fortuitous happening with me, but my permanent, my normal condition, and therefore neither a weakness nor a vice,' cynically confesses the hero of the *Underworld*.

'I am capable of desiring to do something good and of feeling pleasure from it; at the same time, I desire evil and feel pleasure from that, too,' wrote Stavrogin in his last letter. 'I can with perfect convenience experience two opposite feelings at one and the same time, and not of course through my own will,' says Versilov in *A Raw Youth*. Mitya Karamazov puts the case even more poignantly: 'A man with lofty mind and heart begins with the ideal of the Madonna and ends with the ideal of Sodom. What is still more awful is that a man with the ideal of Sodom in his soul does not renounce the ideal of the Madonna, and his heart may be on fire with that ideal, genuinely on fire, just as in his days of youth and innocence. Yes, man is broad, too broad indeed! I'd have him narrower!'

Such an inner split is something more sinister than the so-called 'ambivalence' in modern psychology. It becomes particularly dangerous when it threatens our most vital dilemmas and values. On the other hand, this very danger leads us to a further conclusion, namely, that human personality can only be held together by something that transcends it. Lacking a deeper focus and justification, it falls back upon itself, in which case it either must find an outlet at its own risk, or else disintegrate. One's consciousness may even become self-divided to such an extent as to exclude any consistent decision or act of valuation.

There are, of course, various planes and stages of self-division. In an advanced stage, for example, one's 'second self' may appear in the form of hallucinations, symbolizing urges and impulses which are beyond the grasp of our normal 'Euclidean' understanding. This we can see in Ivan's nightmare. At times another person altogether plays the part of one's *alter ego*, since there are unconscious 'telepathic' contacts the real nature of which has been explored much too little. The relations between the cuckolded Pavel Pavlovitch (in *The Eternal Husband*) and Velchaninov, his dead wife's former lover, is a case in point. The suspicious husband is drawn towards his wife's seducer by a strange magnetism. Yet while solicitously waiting on him during his illness, he attempts—as though in a trance—to murder him. Far-reaching unconscious contacts are those between Raskolnikov and the cynic Svidrigailov (*Crime and Punishment*), between Myshkin and Rogozhin (*The Idiot*), between Stavrogin and Peter Verhovensky (*The Possessed*), between Versilov and Arkady (*A Raw Youth*), between Ivan and the flunkey Smerdyakov (*The Brothers Karamazov*). Other instances are illustrated by presentiments: the confused foreboding of Stavrogin's demented wife Marya; or the monastery scene when the elder Zosima bows to the ground before Mitya Karamazov.

VI

Dostoevsky and Proust are the two great psychologists of disintegration. But whereas Proust dissected this process with the coldness of a peep-hole eavesdropper, remaining all the time on the psycho-biological plane, Dostoevsky's psychology was part and parcel of his own spiritual quest. And as for his intuitive clairvoyance, he owed it to the wide range of his inner life. He owed it also to such extraordinary experiences as the death-sentence in the Semyonovsky Square, or the Siberian katorga. His very self-division was a proof of his chaotic inner wealth which he tried to organize through his art. And contrary to the preachers of healthy normality, he saw in such a state not only a danger, but also the promise of a fuller life—provided our 'duality' and chaos are duly faced and overcome.

In 1880, only a few months before his death, Dostoevsky wrote the following letter to one of his correspondents: 'But now, to what you have told me of your inward duality. That trait is indeed common to all . . . that is, to all who are not wholly commonplace. Nay, it is common to human nature, though it does not evince itself so strongly in all as it does in you. It is precisely on this ground that I cannot but regard you as a twin soul, for your inward duality corresponds most exactly with my own. Such duality means that you have a strong sense of yourself, much aptness of self-criticism, and an innate feeling for your moral duty to yourself and mankind. If your intelligence were less developed, if you were more limited, you would be less sensitive, and would not possess that duality. Rather the reverse: in its stead would have appeared great arrogance. Yet such duality is a great torment.'

Dostoevsky accepted this torment. Most of his efforts to master it, to arrive through the tragedy of self-division at a new unity and integration of his own self, are recorded in his works. It is here that he comes very close to another modern psychologist, C. G. Jung. He would be the first to endorse Jung's statement (in the latter's essay about the differences between Freud and himself): 'We moderns are faced with the necessity of rediscovering the life of the spirit; we must experience it anew for ourselves. It is the only way in which we can break the spell that binds us to the cycle of biological events.'

Dostoevsky's interest in religion, as well as his emphasis on the incompetence of mere intellect as far as man's deepest problems and dilemmas are concerned, is analogous to that of Jung, however much the two may otherwise differ in their approach. One of the best clues to Dostoevsky the psychologist is perhaps provided by this passage from Jung's essay, *The Stages of Life*:[1]

'Do we ever understand what we think? We only understand that thinking which is a mere equation, and from which nothing comes but what we have put in. That is the working of the intellect. But beyond that there is a thinking in primordial images—in symbols which are older than historical man; which have been ingrained in him from earliest times, and, eternally living, outlasting all generations, still make up the groundwork of the human psyche. It is only possible to live the fullest life when we are in harmony with these symbols; wisdom

[1] In *Modern Man in Search of a Soul* (Kegan Paul).

is a return to them. It is neither a question of belief nor of knowledge, but of the agreement of our thinking with the primordial images of the unconscious. They are the source of all our conscious thoughts, and one of these primordial thoughts is the idea of life after death. Science and these symbols are incommensurables. They are indispensable conditions of the imagination; they are primary data—the materials whose expediency and warrant to exist science cannot deny offhand.'

The above passage actually sums up Dostoevsky the author, the thinker, and the psychologist. He did his best to work out his own acceptance of life through the greatest tension between the truth of the intellect and the truth of the 'primordial symbols': a process which became more absorbing the more passionately he endeavoured to extract a final meaning from it all.

IV

THE QUEST OF VALUES

I

EACH individual whose inner growth has not been stopped, is confronted sooner or later by the problem of the meaning of life. As long as he can passively accept the scale of values dictated by the official religion, his social group or class, he is spared the ordeal of a personal quest. This begins only when, in the name of his own independence, he turns the accepted notions about the ultimate things into problems which must be solved from within and at his own risk. In the West the process of individual independence had once been fostered by the wave of the Renaissance and Humanism, whose belated splashes reached Russia only in the eighteenth century, i.e. after the reforms of Peter the Great. In this respect, too, Russia was compelled to make a short cut, amply illustrated by the subsequent evolution of the Russian intelligentsia. And since this short cut reached in Dostoevsky its most dramatic intensity, he presents a phenomenon Europe can hardly ignore in a period of a breakdown such as we are now passing through. His significance is enhanced by the manner in which he approached man's basic dilemmas, and at the same time refused all facile and superficial solutions. He never tired of fighting, and fiercely so, the facile optimism with regard to our progress, for example. Nor was he inclined to make any truce with those theories (whether socialistic or otherwise), the aim of which is to make human beings 'happy' by lowering their consciousness; by standardizing them into mere units of an efficient ant-hill.

His *Notes from the Underworld* was his first protest against such optimistic rationalism. At the same time it was an indirect defence of human personality as something autonomous; something which must insist on its own rights, without isolating itself, however, from the collective group or groups. An individual who remains exclusively in the group, within the sphere of social taboos and conventions, cannot develop into a personality. On the other hand, an isolated personality which has lost its organic contact with the collective or with the rest of mankind, is bound to become starved through its very isolation. The problem of personality thus becomes inseparable from the problem of mankind as a whole. The two are in fact one and the same problem, approached from its opposite ends.

As a brooding modern sceptic, Dostoevsky was familiar with the pride and the torments of isolation. But, having reached its farthest limits (when surrounded by the criminals in Siberia), he also realized man's irrational need of getting out of his own shell and of merging with other fellow beings. This meant to him not to dissolve his own self in the collective group, but to enlarge and to transcend that self. Such an impulse is one of those 'primordial' irrational urges which have found their proper expression in religious images and symbols. Dostoevsky, too, approached it, above all, on a religious plane.

It was here, however, that his main difficulties began. These were due to the fact that he was too much of a sceptic to accept human existence with the spontaneity either of a primitive or of a truly religious man. Unable to accept life spontaneously, he was compelled to take it up as a problem. But life as a problem demands a meaning which must satisfy our rational and irrational selves. At a certain stage the meaning of life may even become more important than life itself. One can reject life altogether, unless its meaning answers to the highest demands of our consciousness.

It is at this stage that a valuation of the whole of

existence, of the actual and the metaphysical order of the world, becomes imperative. The idea of the human ego emerges here in a new 'psychological' light. So does the age-old idea of God and immortality. And both are likely to become inseparable from one's quest of values.

II

These remarks may perhaps explain why so many of Dostoevsky's characters are haunted by the question: 'Does God exist or not?' Dostoevsky himself tackled the problem not on the plane of theological formulae, but primarily as a psychologist interested in God as an active element in man's consciousness—an element which fills the latter not only with the highest longings, but also with the bitterest doubts and torments. 'If I accept the fact that a god is absolute and beyond all human experience, he leaves me cold. I do not affect him, nor does he affect me. But if I know, on the other hand, that God is a mighty activity in my soul, at once I must concern myself with him; he can then become even unpleasantly important, and in practical ways, too, which sounds horribly banal, like everything appearing in the sphere of reality.' —This passage by C. G. Jung (in his commentary to *The Secret of the Golden Flower*) covers Dostoevsky's attitude, but only partly. Unable to separate man's fundamental problems from the problem of God, Dostoevsky was anxious to explore the degree of reality of that 'mighty activity' in our soul. He wanted to know whether God exists also objectively, i.e. apart from and outside that activity. He demanded certainty in this matter mainly in order to see how the answer (one way or the other) would affect the fate of man. The search for God he thus identified primarily with the question as to whether there exists an incontestable, absolute Value towards which one's will and efforts could be directed for the sake of one's highest self-realization and 'way of life'. And since such a Value can only be given or sanctioned by an absolute Being, the answer as to whether God exists or not is bound to affect us. If the latter is in the negative, then our existence—taken not from the social, but from the spiritual angle—is turned into something accidental and devoid of any ultimate meaning. Once cognizant of that, an uncompromising conscience must either reject life and the world, or else proclaim man's will as the only law, and his ego as the only divinity on earth.

'If God exists, all is His will and from His will I cannot escape! If not, it is all my will, and I am bound to show self-will. . . . Because all will has become mine,' says the maniac Kirillov in *The Possessed*. The nightmare devil whispers the same idea to Ivan Karamazov: 'Since there is anyway no God, the new man may well become man-God, even if he is the only one in the world; and promoted to his new position, he may light-heartedly overstep all barriers of the old morality, of the old slave-man, if necessary. Where God stands, the place is holy. . . . "All things are lawful," and that is the end of it.'

From this standpoint morality would be reduced to a matter of customs and taboos, of rules imposed by law, by class conventions and class interests. Instead of a great organism, mankind would be looked upon—at its best—only as a great organization, manipulated by statistics, by economic needs, and by decrees 'aiming at the greatest happiness of the greatest number'. At its worst, however, it would degenerate into an orgy of lust for power and an interminable war of all against all. Devoid of a 'higher idea' which might provide an inner bond between men, humanity would fall a prey to the law of the jungle. And as for the more daring individuals, they would probably feel justified in adopting the attitude, defined by Dostoevsky in one of his letters as follows: 'I need but live my appointed day and let the rest go hang. And if that is really so—and if I am clever enough not to let myself be caught by the standing laws, why should I not kill, rob, steal, or at any rate live at the expense of others? For I shall die, and all the rest will die, and utterly vanish.'

'All things are lawful' thus becomes a negation of values. Instead of the will, directed towards the Value, one only obtains will for will's sake. In the end one is landed in the utter relativity of morals. But on the spiritual plane this simply means a void—that moral void, with its *negative* 'beyond good and evil', into which Raskolnikov had plunged; which had swallowed Svidrigailov, Stavrogin, and had finally threatened to engulf also Ivan Karamazov in whom the paradox of such a dilemma was carried to extreme limits.

The problem goes, however, farther still. If God as a supreme Value and Way of Life does not exist, then the world is a casual complex of blind forces, and man himself an equally casual result of these forces. In whatever he does, he is but their plaything, their puppet, whether he knows it or not. Which means that he is devoid of freedom. Materialist determinism with its 'iron laws of Nature', 'blind Fate', or whatever else we may call it, is a negation of freedom, and consequently a negation of personality. On the other hand, if God exists and 'all is His will', then there is perhaps no freedom either—because there is no room left for man's will. Whatever he wills is actually determined by God. Instead of being a free personality, he is a tool, a puppet of God. Religious determinism (with predestination, etc.) becomes a logical conclusion. The only escape from such an impasse would be the idea of freedom as something existing parallel with God and even independent of Him.

Yet even in accepting this attitude fully, we do not solve the problem of freedom, but turn it into a greater puzzle than ever. The same applies to the problem of Value which cannot be divorced either from the problem of freedom or from the problem of God. There is a line where all three are bound to merge, as Dostoevsky proved it. And since he himself admitted that during the whole of his life he had been 'tormented by God', a brief digression will perhaps help us to find a clue to such torments, so typical of him and of his main characters.

III

Any radical quest of values depends on man's basic attitude towards God and the Universe. This attitude can be twofold. Man either recognizes himself as a component part of all creation and therefore sees his highest goal in a harmony between his own will and the will of God, to which he submits and with which he wishes to merge in an inner, i.e. a mystical union; or else he rejects God (provided he believes in Him) in the name of his own self-will and independence—whether fictitious or real, no matter how big the price.

These two divergent tendencies exist, at least potentially, in every human being. They express, moreover, some ultimate and perhaps necessary cleavage in human consciousness. For even in advanced religions man's purely external 'independent' attitude towards God still remains in some form or other. This is why Professor James H. Leuba warns the reader in his *Psychology of Religious Mysticism* that there are 'two types of religious relation—in the one, it consists in objective, business-like transactions with God; in the other it consists in communion or union with God or even in an absorption in the divine Substance. These two different attitudes, and the different methods of worship they involve, are observable throughout the history of religion, both in private and in public worship. We find them among uncivilized races as clearly as among ourselves. . . . Among Christian nations both the objective and the mystical type of religion are usually found side by side. In the controversy about Quietism, in which Bossuet and Fénélon were the great protagonists and Mme Guyon the victim, Bossuet represents rational Christianity in which man and God—the creature and the Creator, the sinner and the Judge—remain face to face with each other. While Mme Guyon represents Christian mysticism in a form with which common sense could have nothing to do. It is a relation in which the self dissolves in God. The Christian mystics themselves realize clearly enough this dualism. They say that these two attitudes are diametrically contrary to one another.'

Professor Leuba here obviously refers to the contrast between the external legalistic and the inner or mystical attitudes towards God. But this contrast may be carried much farther. The 'legalistic' form, in particular, varies enormously. The primitive man usually tried to bribe the gods (personified forces of Nature), and to exploit them for his own purposes. It was partly to this end that he watched the mysterious phenomena of heaven and earth, and discovered—in the course of time—the first scientific laws. Parallel with that he practised sorcery, magic, and incantations, in order to impose his own will even upon the gods, when necessary. Failing in his attempts to subjugate the 'divine' will to his own, he would humble himself before it like a slave. But in the meantime he would be on the look-out for another chance to assert his own will as far as possible.

A modern counterpart of this 'magical' impulse is Nietzsche's superman, or man-God, as distinct from his opposite: the mystical God-man or Christ. Whereas a mystic enlarges his self to the size of the All, or else dissolves in the All, in God, the 'magical' man-God tends to acquire the power of divinity, or else opposes God Himself as an equivalent entity. Nietzsche expressed this attitude with religious fervour in his *Thus Spake Zarathustra*. Yet the problems involved were tackled with great insight in Dostoevsky's novels long before Nietzsche.

IV

Among the religious teachers it was Christ in particular who abolished the purely legalistic conceptions of God, by transferring Him from outside into the consciousness of man: 'The Kingdom of God is within you.' But this mystical attitude, even when practised whole-heartedly, failed to destroy the rebellious 'magical' element in man, since both attitudes represent the two polar unconscious tendencies of every human self. Hence the duality of man's inner life, and even of mankind's development as a whole. The antagonism between the spiritual and the secular aspects in our historical life may partly be traced back to this split. The latter can occur, however, also on the plane of spirit alone—a phenomenon which often leads to unexpected conflicts, culminating in the antithesis of God-man and man-God, of Christ and Zarathustra.

The inner struggle of Dostoevsky's heroes, from Raskolnikov to Ivan Karamazov, is mainly due to this dilemma and to its two opposite sets of valuation, pushed to their final conclusions. During this process Dostoevsky realized that Christ has revealed to us the highest possible Value. In his opinion 'there is nothing lovelier, deeper, more sympathetic, more manly and perfect than the Saviour'. He even makes his 'superman' Kirillov exclaim that Christ is the One who gave the meaning to life, and that 'the whole planet, with everything in it, is mere madness without that Man'. Yet to see in Christ the Value and the meaning of life is not enough for an inquiring mind. One step farther, and we are confronted by the question: Does Christ Himself correspond to truth? Where is the certainty that the Value and the Way of Life, revealed by Him, are incontestable, with a reality behind, and not a mere illusion? In other words, is Christ Himself inside or outside the Truth?

Supposing we accept Christ as being inside the Truth and regard the Value revealed by Him as incontestable —do we not immediately stumble over another obstacle: the injustice and suffering we see in the world? If God exists, man is bound to judge Him by the world created by Him. Finding in the latter so much misery and injustice, we are entitled to conclude that God (as supreme Wisdom and Reason) either does not exist, or else that He is outside the Value proclaimed by Christ and has nothing to do with it. At a certain stage of consciousness one even can turn against God from *moral indignation*. One can repudiate both Him and His world for *moral* reasons, as did the old Manichaeans and Bogomils who identified the Creator of the visible world with Satan himself and treated him accordingly. How can we then identify Christ and His message with such a God? Which means that Christ Himself may only be a beautiful illusion, a self-delusion, and altogether 'outside the Truth'.

V

Questions of this kind, prompted by incurable scepticism, crop up in all the chief novels of Dostoevsky, not as 'philosophy', but as living experience, as torments of the spirit. They are equally conspicuous in Dostoevsky himself. An atheist and a revolutionary in his twenties, he underwent a change in Siberia. The populist idea with which he came back and for which he worked in his two periodicals, *Vremia* and *Epokha*, had a quasi-mystical flavour. His next phase was to regard the Russian people (less the uprooted intelligentsia) even as a 'god-bearing' nation. Prince Myshkin talks with suspicious fervour of the 'Russian God' who comes to the fore, once again, in Shatov's conversation with Stavrogin (*The Possessed*).

Dostoevsky's final word on God and religion was, of course, different. Yet the stages, leading up to it, are an eloquent proof of both his scepticism and his *will to believe*. He was so much afraid of the inner devastation, caused by modern scepticism, that he fought it with all the means at his disposal. Knowing that he himself was not only a sceptic, but a latent nihilist, he was all the more on his guard against his destructive intellect. In short, he asserted the priority of the irrational over the rational, and began to cling to Christ even in spite of reason. 'If any one could prove to me that Christ is outside the truth, and if the truth really did exclude Christ, I would prefer to stay with Christ and not with the truth,' he confessed candidly. On the other hand, he was too much of a dialectitian and a sharp thinker to be able to accept his religious intuitions without a rational sanction. As the two proved incompatible, he had to fight for his faith, step by step, during the whole of his creative life. 'I want to say to you about myself that I am a child of this age, a child of unfaith and scepticism, and probably—indeed I know it—shall remain so to the end of my life. How dreadfully has it tormented me— and torments me even now—this longing for faith, which is all the stronger for the proofs I have against it,' he wrote to Mme Fonvizin in 1854, during his exile in Siberia. But in 1880, that is, shortly before his death, he gave this advice to one of his correspondents: 'My dear, my revered Mlle N. N., do you believe in Christ and His covenants? If you believe—or if you *desire* very much to believe—then devote yourself to Him, and the torments arising from this inner duality will be considerably relieved; your spirit will be pacified, and this is the main thing . . .' No less eloquent was his statement (during his polemics with K. O. Kavelin) that 'never, even in Europe, had atheism been expressed with such power' as in his own novels. 'I do not believe naïvely as a boy in Christ whom I confess. My hosanna has passed through great whirlwinds of doubt.'

These whirlwinds of doubt were one of the main sources of Dostoevsky's writings. The fight for belief is accompanied in them by the most vigorous apology for unbelief. But for this very reason they are all the more poignant both as literature and as human documents.

THE 'UNDERWORLD' SPIRIT

I

DOSTOEVSKY's hero of *Notes from the Underworld* exclaims jeeringly in his soliloquy: 'So at length, gentlemen, we have reached the conclusion that the best thing for us to do is to do nothing at all, but to sink into a state of contemplative inertia. For that purpose all hail the underworld! True, I said above that I profoundly envy the normal man; yet under the conditions in which I see him placed, I have no wish to be him. Yet I am lying. I am lying because I know that it is not the underworld which is so much better, but something else—something else for which I am hungry, but which I shall never find.'

Offer him happiness, luxury, and comfort—he will laugh. The squalid den, to which he sticks like a crab to its shell, is more to his taste, although he is perfectly aware that his 'underworld' is only a shelter from the actual world with its scramble for existence, its laws of Nature, and all the rest. 'What have I to do,' he asks, 'with the laws of Nature or with arithmetics, when all the time those laws and the formula that twice two make four do not meet with my acceptance? Of course, I am not going to beat my head against a wall if I have not the requisite strength to do so; yet I am not going to accept the wall merely because I have run up against it, and have no means to knock it down.'

Too weak to cope with life and its 'laws', he has become a failure, a nobody, whom people can insult as they like. None the less he asserts his own self even through his impotence. Instead of accepting the 'wall', he protests by retiring into his den. For years he nurses there his rancour, taunting himself with his own humiliation and exaggerating it constantly—lest his passive protest should lose its intensity.

Rejected by the world, he takes revenge by rejecting the world in his turn—deliberately and on principle. In spite of his 'contemplative inertia', his impotent ego challenges (in theory) the entire social order, the whole of Nature and humanity. And through the virulence of this challenge he transforms his weakness into a temporary illusion of strength. The greater his personal frustrations, the stronger grows his spite and defiance through which alone he can assert his own self. Rob him of his suffering, and he will lose his right to protest, i.e. his only delusion of power and self-affirmation on a grand scale. Hence the mere possibility of being pleased with life frightens him. Degradation and shame have become his inner need, his moral need in fact, and the strongest spring of his existence. That is why he revels in his 'underworld'. Secretly he realizes that comfort and happiness would be his undoing. And so he feels 'happy' only when he is unhappy.

Another example of such an attitude is the hysterical Nastasya Filippovna (*The Idiot*) whose injured soul 'had gone to such lengths that it preferred to sit and nurse its contempt and hatred in solitude rather than mount to heights of hitherto unattainable splendour'. She ran away from Myshkin into shame and death because she *did not want* to be happy after all the injuries she had undeservedly suffered. Her rival, Aglaya, sums her up in this cruel diagnosis: 'All you could love was your shame and the perpetual thought that you were disgraced and insulted. If you were less shameful, or had no cause at all for shame, you would be still more unhappy than you are now.' Myshkin, too, agrees that in her 'perpetual admission of guilt (i.e., in her self-laceration and shame) she probably finds some unnatural satisfaction—as though she were revenging herself upon some one'.

Even the Dickensian little Nellie in *The Insulted and*

Injured belongs to the same category of sufferers. 'She had been ill-treated; her hurt could not be healed, and she seemed purposely trying to aggravate her wound, as though she enjoyed her own pain by this *egoism of suffering*, if I may so express it. This aggravation of suffering and this revelling in it I could understand; it is the enjoyment of many of the insulted and injured, oppressed by destiny, and smarting under the sense of its injustice. . . . She seemed trying to astonish and alarm us by her exploits, her caprices and wild pranks, as though she really were asserting herself against us.'

II

If we now transfer this self-assertive and sometimes even ecstatic 'egoism of suffering' (with its secret craving for revenge) to a spiritual and religious plane, we obtain a curious gallery of characters: Dostoevsky's metaphysical rebels, as represented by Raskolnikov in *Crime and Punishment*, the nihilist Ippolit in *The Idiot*, the 'man-God' Kirillov in *The Possessed*, and Ivan Karamazov.

In each of them we see a different stage of revolt. But the feature they all have in common is their challenge to the entire world-order, or the world-will if you like, which they regard as devoid of Value. They differ, however, in their conception of this Will. A rebel who suspects God behind the Universe may rise against Him either for over-personal or else for personal reasons. In both cases he turns into a 'God-struggler'—to use a word which is frequent in modern Russian philosophy. If, however, he feels behind it only a 'dark Power', a senseless complex of blind forces, he becomes what might be called a cosmic nihilist.

'If God exists, all is His will and from His will I cannot escape!' exclaims the God-struggler. Nevertheless his conscience rebels against God when, instead of Value and the ultimate meaning of life, he finds in Him mere tyrannical will, victimizing the world and mankind. He

opposes God's will by his own *independent* will—whether
actual or illusory, no matter what the consequences of
such a protest may be. The height of moral indignation,
underlying this protest is expressed by the notorious
dictum: 'If God existed, He ought to be killed!'

Equally indignant can be the reaction against the 'dark
Power'. The main stages of such a reaction are indicated
in Ippolit's confession (which he reads before his tragi-
comic attempt to commit suicide). Amongst other things,
Nature appears to him 'as some huge implacable, dumb
monster, or, still better, some enormous mechanical engine
of modern days. . . . I thought some one led me by the
hand and showed me, by the light of a candle, a huge,
loathsome insect, which he assured me was that very
force, that very almighty, dumb, irresistible Power, and
laughed at the indignation with which I received this
information. It was impossible for me to go on living
when life was full of such detestable, strange, tormenting
forms. Nor could I bear to be subordinate to that dark,
horrible force which was embodied in the form of the
loathsome insect. If I had the power to prevent my own
birth I should certainly never have consented to accept
existence under such ridiculous conditions. However, I
have the power to end my existence, although I do but
give back days that are already numbered. It is an
insignificant gift, and my revolt is equally insignificant.'

Similarly, Kirillov in *The Possessed* bases his own revolt
and suicide on the assumption that 'all the planet is a
lie and rests on a lie and on mockery. So then, the very
laws of the planet are a lie and the vaudeville of devils. . . .'
'As I find this comedy stupid, unbearable, and insulting,
I sentence this Nature—which created me insolently only
to make me suffer—to disappear with me. As I cannot
carry out my sentence in the whole by destroying Nature
together with myself, I must destroy myself at least, and
so be rid of a tyranny for which no one is responsible,'
declares another rebel of this kind in *The Sentence*, a

remarkable psychological document in *The Journal of an Author*.

Ivan Karamazov goes even farther in his accusations and his demand of justice. He acknowledges the possibility of God's existence, but at the same time refuses to see in Him the Value and to accept the world created by Him. A diabolical world, such as the one we live in, is more likely to be the work of devils than of a just and wise God. Even if a real 'Kingdom of God', full of harmony, should be the outcome of all the past and present suffering, Ivan's outraged moral sense would refuse happiness and harmony paid for by the untold misery of past generations. 'It is not that I don't accept God, it is the world created by Him I don't and cannot accept. Even if parallel lines do meet and I see it myself, I shall see it and say that they have met, but still I won't accept it. I don't want harmony. *From love for humanity* —I don't want it. I would rather remain with my un-avenged suffering and unsatisfied indignation, *even if I were wrong*.'[1]

The 'magical' impulse, combined with a supreme sense of justice, thus asserts itself against the cosmic will as the latter's judge, as its equal. But 'if God exists, all is His will and from His will I cannot escape', however much I protest. I could evade His (or the 'dark Power's') tyranny only by destroying Him. As this is impossible, I have but one alternative left—to destroy myself. I can show the climax of my illusory self-assertion through self-destruction which is at the same time the final act of my 'non-obedience', of my 'new, terrible liberty', as Kirillov calls it. 'I have always been surprised at every one's going on living,' he declares before his suicide. 'Can it be that no one in the whole planet, after making an end of God and believing in his own self-will, will dare to express his self-will on the most vital point? It is like a beggar inheriting a bag of gold, thinking himself

---

[1] Italics are mine.

too weak to own it. I want to manifest my self-will. I may be the only one, but I'll do it. I am bound to shoot myself because the highest point of my self-will is to kill myself by my own hands.'

There is, of course, no certainty that by suicide one really destroys oneself. One's consciousness may continue to exist in some other dispensation which is perhaps even more outrageous and senseless than the world it has rejected. Svidrigailov (*Crime and Punishment*) puts it rather figuratively: 'We always imagine eternity as something beyond our conception, something vast, vast! But why must it be vast? Instead of all that, what if it's only one little room, like a bath-house in the country, black and grimy and spiders in every corner, and that's all eternity is? I sometimes fancy it like that.' But such a state would only increase one's rebellion, even if it should last eternally.

III

The protest we have just analysed takes place not so much for one's own sake as from a Promethean love of humanity, and in the name of humanity. 'I must have justice, or I will destroy myself. And not justice in some remote time and space, but here on earth and that I could see myself,' claims Ivan Karamazov.

But a protest of the same kind is also possible exclusively for one's own sake. In this case the individual wants to avenge the 'insult' of his personal existence on God, on His world, on everybody and everything. The God-struggler, who demands an account for the last suffering creature, is thus replaced by the 'satanist' who is himself ready to torture and to destroy if he can thereby assert his defiant self-will against God. The more he is aware of his own nothingness and impotence, the more hysterical becomes his mania to serve the destructive Satanic principle of life and spirit. Sadism on the one hand, and blasphemy on the other, are the chief vehicles of such a disposition. The two phenomena are inwardly allied: what may be mere sadistic cruelty on the psychological plane, becomes blasphemy and sacrilege on the plane of spirit. Such a blasphemer finds his joy in trampling down everything sacred—a practice which he often pushes to the farthest limits of imagination. Crimes, sacrilege, and the lowest depravity (derived not from physiological, but from spiritual and 'moral' sensuality) are the vehicles of his self-will. The awareness that he is defying God Himself, and that he is a castaway for all eternity not through God's will, but through his own *independent* will—through his 'new, terrible liberty', turns into a source of pride and of a perverse spiritual ecstasy which cannot even be comphrended by an irreligious sceptical age such as ours. The medieval Witches' Sabbath with its grossly blasphemous rites may have been prompted, to some extent, by such impulses. Obsessed by self-will, by his urge to destroy everything —including God, a true satanist laughs at the very mention of inner peace, happiness, and contentment. He would not give up his rebellion even if he saw clearly that it was he himself, and not God, who was wrong.

'Oh, there are some who remain fierce and proud even in hell, in spite of their certain knowledge and contemplation of absolute truth; there are some fearful ones who have given themselves over to Satan and to his proud spirit entirely. For such, hell is voluntary and everconsuming; they are tortured by their own choice. For they have cursed themselves, cursing God and life. They live upon their vindictive pride like a starving man in the desert sucking blood out of his own body. But they are never satisfied, they refuse forgiveness, they curse God who calls them. They cannot behold the living God without hatred, and they cry out that the God of life should destroy Himself and His own creation. And they burn in the fire of their own wrath for ever.'

These words of Father Zosima (*The Brothers Karamazov*) are perhaps the best spiritual counterpart to the statement of the Underworld man: 'Whence do savants have it that man needs a normal, a virtuous will? What, in particular, has made these pundits imagine that what man most needs is a will which is acutely alive to man's interests? Why, what man most needs is an *independent* will—no matter what the cost of such independence of volition, nor what it may lead to!' But let us now consider another aspect of such an independent will.

IV

One of the phenomena, inherent in the satanic self-assertion just mentioned, is the reversal of moral instincts and values. The impulse to defy God expands into a craving for evil, for all that is abnormal, perverted and ugly. Each value is turned inside-out: not from a puerile quest for 'new emotions' (as was the case with the decadents two generations ago), but from an inner need to destroy and to blaspheme. The famous Categorical Imperative thus becomes inverted: it degenerates into an imperative for evil.

So we reach the meeting point of the satanist and the 'transcendental criminal' (a cumbersome word, used for the first time by Otto Weininger).[1] There is no doubt that such criminals do exist, whatever their actual occupations may be. For in the same manner as the preponderance of the mystical element can lead towards saintliness, the complete sway of the 'magical' impulse turns one into a transcendental criminal, who may be defined as a latent satanist. In him the Categorical imperative is turned inside-out: good he construes as evil, and evil as good. Such an attitude can remain unconscious, but even so it is sinister enough and fundamentally different from the irresponsible 'moral imbecility', although what we call repentance may be equally foreign to it.

Dostoevsky, from whom criminology has a good deal

[1] Modern criminology would simply call him an 'instinctive criminal'.

to learn in this respect, writes in his *House of the Dead* that among his fellow-convicts in Siberia he had known 'murderers who were so gay and free from care that one might have made a bet their conscience never made them the least reproach'. A pronounced specimen of the sort was a certain Orlov—'a malefactor of a rare kind, capable of assassinating in cold blood old men and children. He possessed an indomitable force of will, and was fully conscious of his power. When he understood that I was endeavouring to see through him, and to discover in him some trace of repentance, he looked at me with a haughty and contemptuous air, as if I were a foolish little boy, to whom he did too much honour by conversing with him. I detected in his countenance a sort of compassion for me. After a minute's pause he laughed out loud, but without the least irony. I fancy he must, more than once, have laughed in the same manner, when my words returned to his memory. In reality he must have despised me, for I was a feeble being, contemptible in all respects, and guilty above all of resignation.'

The so-called demoniac characters are often transcendental criminals in disguise. Sometimes they become irresponsible sadists, sometimes murderers, sometimes great conquerors, or even great artists. Art certainly is one of the channels through which such 'cruel' dispositions can be sublimated. Dostoevsky must have known this from his own experience, since he created characters such as Svidrigailov, Stavrogin, the old Karamazov. But his case was complicated by the fact that the two antagonistic impulses were active in him at one and the same time. He rebelled against God in the name of Satan, and against Satan in the name of God simultaneously. And in doing this, he still remained too much of a 'child of unfaith' to believe fully in either of them. The struggle for his own Hosanna was thus long and painful. His chief characters, from Raskolnikov onwards, are but milestones on his journey through man's spiritual 'underworld'.

VI

THE BANKRUPTCY OF THE SUPERMAN

I

IT is significant that the first post-Siberian work which brought general recognition to Dostoevsky is called *Crime and Punishment*. This novel is not devoid of lapses into melodrama, or of somewhat forced coincidences, yet as a whole it is a great achievement. Dostoevsky tackled in it the psychology and the problem of crime. What engrossed him, and absorbingly so, was neither the legal nor the social, but the spiritual nature of crime. And as for punishment, he scrutinized it only in terms of the inner reaction to the crime on the part of the transgressor himself.

Rodión Raskolnikov (the hero of the novel) is the first of Dostoevsky's characters in whom the problem of crime and the problem of Value intertwine. But since Raskolnikov's deed takes place before a satisfactory explanation has been given, the reader remains in the dark for a while as to the actual motive or motives of the planned murder. Did that half-starved student kill the pawnbroker woman from poverty? From a desire to relieve the financial worries of his mother and sister? Or in order to shape with the stolen money his own future on a big scale, to redeem his crime by becoming a benefactor to mankind? Was there at the bottom of it the gnawing vanity of a maniac who wanted to gain power and to be one of the mighty, perhaps a new Napoleon? Or was it primarily the spiritual recklessness of a youth who dared to over-step the 'herd-morality', the old boundaries of good and evil, in order to test the strength of his own defiance?

What transpires even from the early chapters of the novel is the fact that Raskolnikov himself is not entirely sure as to the chief motive of his crime. He, too, is a split personality, divided all the time between the most contradictory impulses and actions. According to a letter he wrote to Katkov, Dostoevsky first wanted Raskolnikov to commit the crime from a generous humanitarian motive. Gradually, however, the stress was shifted upon the 'idea', that is, upon the spiritual ravages caused by one's scornful 'beyond good and evil' attitude. That this is really so can be gathered from one of the meetings between Raskolnikov and Porfiry, whose methods of investigation probably reflect Dostoevsky's own experiences during the Petrashevsky trial in 1849.

In the course of their conversation Porfiry mentions an article in which Raskolnikov anticipated—by several years—the main thesis of Nietzsche. According to that article, mankind is divided by nature into two categories. The first consists of the conservative majority who live and must live in obedience, since they are incapable of living otherwise. The second comprises, however, exceptional men: the daring, commanding and (when necessary) even criminal creators of new values. The true leaders of humanity, great rulers and legislators, can be found in the second group only. And their chief mark is a complete lack of respect for any 'sacred' laws, traditions and morals observed by the community, by the herd. They do not hesitate to break any law or laws obstructing their own ambitions, to which they are ready to sacrifice in cold blood millions of human beings. 'It is remarkable,' Raskolnikov explains, 'that the majority of these benefactors and leaders of humanity were guilty of terrible carnage. In short, I maintain that all great men or even men a little out of the common, that is to say, capable of giving some new word, must from their very nature be criminals—more or less, of course. Otherwise it is hard for them to get out of the common rut; and to remain in the common rut is what they cannot submit to, from their very nature again, and to my mind they ought not, indeed, to submit to it. . . . If such a one is forced for the sake of his idea to step over a corpse or wade through blood, he can, I maintain, find within himself—in his conscience, a sanction for wading through blood—that depends on the idea and its dimensions.'

'What is really *original* in all this, and is exclusively your own, to my horror, is that you sanction bloodshed *in the name of conscience*, and, excuse my saying so, with such fanaticism,' remarked his friend Razumihin. 'But that sanction of bloodshed *by conscience* is to my mind more terrible than the official, legal sanction of bloodshed.'

II

From this one can guess that Raskolnikov is an inflated egotist: a would-be 'superman' who wants to assert his personality by overstepping the values of good and evil and thus prove to himself that he is an exception, a lawgiver, a new Napoleon.[1] With such an ambition in his mind, he chooses murder as his expedient—that is, the very crime through which one human being can assert a maximum of self-will and power over another human being. But Raskolnikov happens to be also a new variety of the brooding 'underworld-man'. He is a Hamlet, who dreams of becoming Napoleon and is not quite sure as yet whether he is entitled to cherish such ambitions or not. It was not his strength, but his lack of strength, or rather his doubt of it, that drove him to the crime. He wanted to prove to himself that he was able to 'take the daring'—to send the old moral values flying, and bravely face the principle of 'all things are lawful'.

The curious point about it was that his logic did not raise any objections. 'Since there is anyway no God, the new man may well become man-God, and promoted to his new position, he may lightheartedly overstep all the

[1] Attention has been drawn to the fact that Raskolnikov is slightly reminiscent of Balzac's Rastignac (*Le Pere Goriot*) and of Lucien de Rubempré in *Les Illusions Perdues*.

barriers of the old morality, of the old slave-man, if necessary.' This prompting of Ivan's nightmare devil found in Raskolnikov its first exponent. Yet in spite of the sanction on the part of his logic, he was troubled and hesitating. Thus after his hideous symbolic dream, in which drunken peasants had beaten to death an old horse, Raskolnikov awoke in horror at the mere idea of his criminal design. Once again he began to doubt whether he could accomplish it at all. 'But what am I going on like this for? I knew that I could never bring myself to it, so what have I been torturing myself for till now?' . . . During his walk along the Neva his load was lifted from his heart. But when he heard, in a chance conversation, that his intended victim would be alone in her flat at a certain time, his obsession got hold of him once again. All freedom of action was gone. He felt like a tool of another mysterious will, which seemed to have decided everything for him. As one in delirium, he then murdered the old pawnbroker woman, and (against his will) also her gentle half-witted sister who had returned to the flat at the moment of the crime. And here began the second act of Raskolnikov's drama.

Dostoevsky unfolds it with uncanny intuition. To begin with, he shows that Raskolnikov's reaction to the crime was not one of remorse, but a vague half-conscious mood which gradually undermined him from underneath as it were. 'If it had been possible to escape to some solitude, he would have thought himself lucky, even if he had to spend his whole life there. But although he had almost always been by himself of late, he had never been able to feel alone. Sometimes he walked out of the town on the high road, but the lonelier the place was the more he seemed aware of an uneasy presence near him. It did not frighten him, but greatly annoyed him, so that he made haste to return to the town, to mingle with the crowd, to enter restaurants and taverns, to walk in busy thoroughfares. . . . Yet he felt that that was not the only cause of his uneasiness; there was something requiring immediate decision, but it was something he could not clearly understand or put into words. It was a hopeless tangle.'

This 'something' became clearer when his old Hamlet-like doubts returned, trailing behind them a retrospective contemplation of his crime. Yet what now oppressed him was not the crime itself, but the mean and loathsome way in which it had happened. Where was the feeling of strength and 'freedom' of a 'superman' who had dared assert his self-will in the teeth of all the moral notions of the 'herd'? He felt instead only disgust and the awareness of being a failure, perhaps even a despicable nonentity who had no right to take such a step.

'I wanted to find out then and quickly whether I was a louse like everybody else or a man. Whether I can step over the barriers or not, whether I am a trembling creature or whether I have the right.' . . . This is how he complained to the innocent prostitute Sonia after the crime. At the same time he knew full well that a man doubting his own right and power is not entitled to have either. A strong man goes straight to his goal, without asking questions. How could a Hamlet ever become Napoleon? 'No, those men are not made so. The real *Master* to whom all is permitted storms Toulon, makes massacre in Paris, *forgets* an army in Egypt, wastes half a million men in the Moscow expedition and gets off with a jest at Vilna. And altars are set up to him after his death, and so *all* is permitted. No, such people it seems are not of flesh, but of bronze! . . . Napoleon, the pyramids, Waterloo, and a wretched skinny old woman, a pawn-broker with a red trunk under her bed. . . . A Napoleon creep under an old woman's bed! Ugh, how loathsome!'

III

Raskolnikov's torment was not one of moral remorse. His loathing of himself and of his deed was above all aesthetic. 'A Napoleon creep under an old woman's bed!'[1] This feeling was increased by his suspicion that in spite of his 'all things are lawful', he himself was a weakling, one of the herd which he despised. While his theoretical reason was beyond good and evil, he was yet compelled to stop on this side of it, without knowing exactly why. The only thing he was aware of was his weakness and self-disgust. Even this burden was too much for him: he had to share it with a hapless prostitute. 'Oh, Sonia! I want to prove one thing only, that the devil led me on then and he has shown me since that I had not the right to take that path, because I am just such a louse like all the rest. He was mocking me and here I've come to you now! Welcome your guest! If I were not a louse, should I have come to you? . . . Did I murder the old woman? I murdered myself, not her! I crushed myself once for all, for ever.'

Had he murdered the old woman only for money and had he failed, his stake would have been trifling in comparison with this sudden crumbling down of all his 'independent volition'. Having asserted his self-will in such a revolting manner at the expense of another person's life, Raskolnikov's was now unable either to remain on this side of good and evil (since he did not believe in its validity), or to go beyond it. He was thus thrown into a spiritual vacuum which he was unable to bear by his very nature. Porfiry was right in defining him as one of those men who 'would stand and smile at their torturer, while he cuts their entrails out, if only to have found their faith or God'.

He needed faith, a value and a 'principle', in order to be able to live at all. It was for the sake of a principle (the 'supra-human' beyond good and evil) that he had

[1] In the deleted chapters of *Stavrogin's Confession* Father Tikhon says: 'There are truly ugly crimes. Crimes whatever they may be, the more blood, the more horror in them, the more imposing, they are, so to say, more picturesque. But there are crimes shameful, disgraceful, past all horror, they are, so to say, almost too inelegant.'

undertaken his crime. But in killing the old woman, he killed also the principle itself as far as he was concerned. 'The old woman was a mistake, but she is not what matters! The old woman was only an illness. . . . I was in a hurry to overstep. . . . I didn't kill a human being, but a principle! I killed the principle, but I didn't over-step, I stopped on this side. . . . I was only capable of killing. And it seems I wasn't even capable of that. . . . Eh, I am an aesthetic louse and nothing more. . . . And what shows that I am utterly a louse is that I am perhaps viler and more loathsome than the louse I killed, and *I felt beforehand* that I should tell myself so *after* killing her. Can anything be compared with the horror of that! The vulgarity! The abjectness! I understand the "prophet" with his sabre, on his steed: Allah commands and trembling creation must obey! The "prophet" is right, when he sets a battery across the street and blows up the innocent and guilty without deigning to explain! It's for you to obey, trembling creation, and not to *have desires*, for that's not for you!'

In his inner vacuum he now discovered yet another kind of irrational 'punishment': his crime had cut him off from all living beings, as though he were a dead limb. A wall had grown up between him and the rest of mankind, including his mother and sister. In his utter isolation, in his 'eternity on a square yard of space', he had thought of suicide, but unlike his *alter ego* Svidrigailov, he was too weak for such an issue. He had killed the old woman physically, but the old woman killed him in return—not physically, but spiritually. He moved about like one dead, and he knew it. At the same time his logic and reason remained as unperturbed and persuasive as before. . . . 'I shall never, never forgive the old woman!'

In a nightmare he actually tried to kill her again, just to take revenge upon her. He struck her skull with the axe, blow on blow, but she hardly stirred. He then bent down to look at her, bent lower, peeped into her face and noticed with horror that the 'old woman was sitting and laughing, shaking with noiseless laughter, doing her utmost that he should not hear it. . . . He was overcome with frenzy and began hitting the old woman on the head with all his force, but at every blow of the axe the laughter grew louder and the old woman was simply shaking with mirth.'

So much for Raskolnikov's experiment with the 'beyond good and evil'.

IV

There were only two human beings with whom this bankrupt superman was still able to feel a certain contact after the murder. Both had something in common with him. One of them was the cynic Svidrigailov, and the other—the prostitute Sonia.

Svidrigailov was partly anticipated by Dostoevsky in Prince Valkovsky's (*The Insulted and Injured*) self-indulgent materialism: 'All is for me; the whole world is created for me. . . . I say one must look at the thing from the simplest, most practical point of view. I, for instance, have long since freed myself from all shackles, and even obligations.'

Svidrigailov belongs to the same category. But like Raskolnikov he, too, must have philosophized away and 'destroyed everything, till he had nothing left', not even the elementary distinction between good and evil. In order to escape from despair, he tried to fill his own vacuum with profligacy which Raskolnikov would have dreaded even had he found in it a temporary shelter from himself. Yet Svidrigailov's 'gay' cynicism is of a sinister, tragic kind. One feels that what is most terrible in him has remained unsaid. He also shows a split mind, and his moral irresponsibility does not exclude generous actions at times. A deliberate card-sharper with regard to fate, he puts everything at stake when in love with Raskolnikov's sister Dounia. And having lost, he shoots himself with that jeering coolness which would be unthinkable in such a weakling as Raskolnikov.

The meek and resigned Sonia provides the greatest contrast to Svidrigailov. But she, too, is a criminal in a way: she murdered her own self through her goodness—in becoming a prostitute for the sake of those whom she loved. 'We two are equally cursed, so our path is the same, even if we look in different directions,' Raskolnikov says to her in an earlier draft for the novel. Sonia, her father—the pathetic drunkard Marmeladov, the hysterical Katerina Ivanovna and her children, form the background of the 'insulted and injured'. And Sonia's self-sacrifice for their sake looks ghastly, in spite of its greatness. She is a symbol of senseless, unnecessary and yet for some reason unavoidable injustice meted out by life. Raskolnikov indicated this when he fell at Sonia's feet, 'bowing down to all the suffering of humanity'.

Yet there was not a sign of rebellion in her. She accepted her lot without grumbling, and never faltered in her naïve Christian faith which was her only solace and shelter. She killed her body in prostituting it, but spiritually she remained alive. And so, apart from Svidrigailov, she was the only person able to understand Raskolnikov the murderer, without condemning him. That was why he clung to her. In the very teeth of his logic he even hoped, half-consciously, that a humble faith such as hers might perhaps still save him from living death; that with her help he might be able to go back to that faith—the faith of the herd—and thus find at least a shelter and a bond with the rest of mankind. Raskolnikov went 'back' to Sonia and listened, in her tiny room, to her reading about the resurrection of Lazarus, although logically he did not believe either in crime, or in moral resurrection. Even when, partly on Sonia's advice—he had decided to hand himself over to the law and to accept suffering, his rebellious 'double' saw in the committed crime only an abject failure and the tragi-comedy of a puffed-up nonentity. Yet he could not help fleeing away from himself and from that void which was his most terrible punishment. In the end he did not mind what happened. 'If I must drink the cup what difference does it make? The more revolting the better.' In his quest for a shelter he was driven, in spite of his reason, to the punishment prescribed by law. He accepted it in the hope that the burden of his inner void might be lifted by suffering. At the same time he loathed all those who would punish him or witness his punishment. Even when on the point of surrender, he said to his sister Dounia:

'I am going to give myself up. But I don't know why I am going to give myself up.'

'Aren't you half expiating your crime by facing the suffering!'

'Crime? What crime?' he cried in sudden fury. 'That I killed a vile noxious insect, an old pawnbroker woman, of use to no one! . . . Killing her was atonement for forty sins. She was sucking the life out of the poor people. Was that a crime? I am not thinking of it and am not thinking of expiating it, and why are you all rubbing it in on all sides? A crime! A crime! Only now I see clearly the imbecility of my cowardice, now that I have decided to face this superfluous disgrace. It's simply because I am contemptible and have nothing in me that I have decided to, perhaps too for my advantage. . . . I am farther than ever from seeing that what I did was a crime. . . . But I wonder shall I in those fifteen or twenty years (of penal servitude) grow so meek that I shall humble myself before people and whimper at every word that I am a criminal. Yes, that's it, that's it, that's what they are sending me there for, that's what they want. Look at them running to and fro about the streets, every one of them a scoundrel and a criminal at heart and, worse still, an idiot. But try to get me off and they'd be wild with righteous indignation. Oh, how I hate them all!'

V

Raskolnikov accepted the punishment by law. He faced the hardships of penal servitude, probably hoping they would provide an escape from himself. But his vacuum persisted. He craved for remorse with which to fill it, but in vain. 'If only fate would have sent him repentance—burning repentance that would have torn his heart and robbed him of sleep, that repentance the awful agony of which brings visions of hanging and drowning! Oh, he would have been glad of it! Tears and agonies would at least have been life. But he did not repent of his crime. . . .' On the rational plane of logic and reason there was nothing he could reproach himself with except failure and weakness. The disturbance came mainly from the realms of the irrational, and here the truth of his logic was utterly helpless.

True enough, the presence of Sonia (who had followed him to the *katorga*) might look like an augury of Raskolnikov's 'resurrection' in accordance with her faith. The reader remains, however, doubtful in spite of Dostoevsky's promise to write another story about it—which he never did. On the other hand, in the Epilogue to *Crime and Punishment* the author made one more attempt to discredit the competence of mere 'logic and reason' with regard to fundamental problems of life. Raskolnikov's allegoric dream during his illness in Siberia states the matter plainly. He dreamt that the entire world had been swept away by a new plague which came from Asia. Some curious new microbes, endowed with intelligence and will, attacked all human beings who at once went mad— from self-will, combined with an excess of science and reason. 'Never had men considered themselves so intellectual and so completely in possession of the truth as these sufferers, never had they considered their decisions, their scientific conclusions, their moral convictions so infallible. Whole villages, whole towns and peoples went mad from the infection. All were excited and did not understand one another. Each thought that he alone had the truth. They did not know how to judge and could not agree what to consider evil and what good; they did not know whom to blame, whom to justify. Men killed each other in a sort of senseless spite. . . . They accused one another, fought and killed each other. There were conflagration and famine. All men and all things were involved in destruction. The plague spread and moved farther and farther.'

This prophetic dream of our present 'brave new world', with its inner and external anarchy, links up the Raskolnikov theme to Dostoevsky's subsequent works. For he returned to it again and again, each time showing some of its further implications.

VII

A RUSSIAN DON QUIXOTE

IN *Crime and Punishment* Dostoevsky dramatized the spiritual paradox of 'beyond good and evil'. Always inclined to think and to work in terms of antinomies, he followed up the dilemma by another novel, *The Idiot*, in which he showed the opposite of Raskolnikov. Judging by his preliminary notes and drafts, it took a considerable time before this novel assumed the shape we know. Its chief character, Prince Myshkin, is the nearest approach to a Christian in Dostoevsky's sense. He is also a Russian equivalent of Don Quixote, reminiscent not so much of the Spanish model as of Ivan the Fool—the wise simpleton of the Russian fairy-tales.

Myshkin is a *tour de force* of characterization. Static and passive, he yet remains the centre of events which keep on increasing both in pace and number, until the final catastrophe overpowers him. During all that period he never shows a backbone or a will of his own, but is swayed either by the impulses of his over-sensitive heart, or else by his childlike, even childish trustfulness. Absence of character thus seems to be his chief characteristic. Yet the entire novel revolves around him. Moreover, with all his meekness, he is neither maudlin nor sentimental. His spontaneous warmth and sympathy save him from that. We also learn at the very outset that he is an epileptic, thoroughly familiar with the irrational experiences this malady often implies.

It is not by chance that Myshkin is introduced to us while returning to Russia from a Swiss sanatorium for the mentally deficient. He himself makes no secret of his former condition. At a closer inspection we see, however, that in spite of his 'idiocy' (from a narrow intellectual standpoint) there is something in him which makes him wiser, more profound, than all the cunning and clever people by whom he is surrounded on his arrival in Petersburg. It looks as though Dostoevsky wanted to show that true intelligence may be something different from, or even hostile to, the mere reasoning intellect. One of the heroines (Aglaya) expresses this clearly, when remarking to Myshkin: 'If anybody says that your mind is sometimes affected, you know—it is unfair. Even if your surface mind be a little affected, yet your real mind is far better than all theirs put together. Such a mind as they have never dreamed of, because really, there are two minds—the kind that matters and the kind that does not matter.' . . . Dominated exclusively by 'the mind that matters', Myshkin relies on his spontaneous flashes of intuition. And his innate sympathy with all life makes him penetrate into the deepest secrets of men almost as a matter of course. His clairvoyance is that of a child to whom mysteries disclose themselves precisely because he never makes the slightest effort to force them. They just come to him. With his preponderance of the irrational, he embodies the quietist-mystical side of Dostoevsky, without Dostoevsky's sceptical 'double'.

II

There is something reminiscent of Kaspar Hauser in the way Prince Myshkin is suddenly ushered into a world for which he is not adapted at all. Owing to his passivity, he is not even tragic, but only pathetic. And when the strain of his experiences becomes too much for him, his mind breaks down once again, this time past recovery. It is only during a short period that we are allowed to watch his reactions to people who baffle him and, in their turn, are baffled by him. In order to make these reactions as varied as possible, Dostoevsky confronts Myshkin with several social layers from princes and generals to nondescript riff-raff. He also piles upon him, without mercy, external and inner calamities which eventually pass far beyond his control. Myshkin becomes an involuntary centre of action, although he himself never acts. On the other hand, he emanates a kind of psychic radiance which seems to infect his surroundings. Even those who despise and exploit him, end by loving him as though under the spell of a charm they would be at a loss to explain.

We meet him for the first time in the train, where he introduces himself to the distressingly 'broad' Rogozhin. A few hours later we see him in the family of General Epanchin. Scrutinized by the incomparable Lizaveta Prokofyevna, he is here made fun of by her three daughters the youngest of whom, Aglaya, is destined to play a memorable part in the novel. On the same day we accompany him to the boarding-house of the Ivolgins with its queer inmates, and in the evening to the flat of the hysterical *dame aux camélias* and Rogozhin's obsession —Nastasya Filippovna. Without the slightest effort or intention, Myshkin makes a complete break in Nastasya's life. In his own way he even falls in love with her. But Nastasya, who had been outraged by her respectable 'protector' Totsky, is too much in love with her own pain and insult to be able to love anybody or anything else. Having run away from Totsky to the uncouth Rogozhin, she runs a few weeks later from Rogozhin to Myshkin, then back to Rogozhin, and again to Myshkin. Myshkin's life becomes all the more muddled, because he is in love also with Aglaya: a strange triangle which leads to strange happenings. Aglaya plays a hide-and-seek game with him. But a truly 'Dostoevskian' interlude with the young nihilists, who make an attempt to blackmail Myshkin (now heir to a fortune), is followed by signs of Aglaya's affection. The two would have become betrothed but for the society party at the Epanchins, spoilt by Myshkin's tactlessness and a sudden epileptic fit. There follows a meeting between Aglaya and Nastasya during which the two rivals contemptuously abuse each other in Myshkin's presence. The moment of decision comes, and his wavering seals his own fate. Unable to forgive him that, swayed by pity, he stands by Nastasya, Aglaya makes a hurried exit from the scene itself, as well as from Myshkin's life.

Nastasya and Myshkin now come together once more. Rogozhin, who has served as an involuntary link between the two, is tormented by sullen and maddening jealousy. There are strange unconscious ties not only between him and Nastasya, but also between him and Myshkin: ties which blend these three lives into one single destiny as it were. Rogozhin is drawn at times towards Myshkin by flashes of almost brotherly affection, but a little later he wants to murder him. Both impulses are parallel in him and equally sincere. There is always something ominous in Rogozhin's behaviour, particularly when Nastasya is with Myshkin. He prowls about like a wounded animal. As though fascinated by the danger in store for her, Nastasya flirts with her own ruin and joins him again and again. Even on the day of her projected marriage to Myshkin, when—resplendent in all her beauty and finery —she drives at last to the wedding, she succumbs to the fascination of horror without being able to resist it. She disappears with Rogozhin, vaguely foreboding what awaits her.

The last pages, dealing with Myshkin's anxious search for his bride, as well as his breakdown in Rogozhin's house (by the body of Nastasya and her delirious murderer), are among the greatest and most gruesome Dostoevsky ever wrote. But this is the final stage of Prince Myshkin's ordeal. His mind becomes clouded again and for good. 'When, after many hours, the door was opened and people thronged in, they found the murderer unconscious and in a raging fever. The prince was sitting by him, and each time that the sick man gave a laugh, or a shout, he hastened to pass his own trembling hand over his companion's hair and cheeks, as though trying to soothe and quiet him, and recognized none of those who surrounded him. If Schneider himself had arrived then and seen his former pupil and patient, remembering the prince's condition during the first year in Switzerland, he would have flung up his hands despairingly, and cried as he did then: "An idiot!"'

III

The majority of the characters in this novel are unusual but fully alive. They are also balanced one with the other in a rather complex pattern. Thus Myshkin's antipodes on the irrational plane is Rogozhin. He is a welter of primary undisciplined passion, which he is unable to master and is therefore mastered by it to the extent of becoming its blind tool, its medium. The two men are drawn towards each other as opposites. And the contrast between them comes best out in their love for Nastasya. Rogozhin's passion reaches the point at which sexual love passes into extreme hatred, into a mania to possess and destroy. Myshkin's love, on the other hand, is sexless pity. He clings to Nastasya mainly in order to save her from herself and—from Rogozhin. For he is aware of Rogozhin's subconscious intentions. Rogozhin vaguely suspects it and tries to get rid of him, partly for this very reason.

Nastasya Filippovna represents the climax of what Dostoevsky called the 'egoism of suffering'. She is the female counterpart of the self-lacerating 'underworld spirit' at its intensest. Seduced and insulted by Totsky, she has turned her fury even against sex. Unable to take revenge on her seducer, she takes revenge upon herself. And her self-humiliation is but her reversed pride. She must have been as much in love with her chastity before, as she is now in love with her pain and disgust. Deriving from the latter a perverted satisfaction, she is no longer an erotic, but a spiritual masochist. In the end her masochism degenerates into a blind will to self-destruction which she instinctively seeks and yet abhors, as is shown by her wavering between Rogozhin and Myshkin.

Nastasya's revolt against sex is one of the reasons for her attachment to Myshkin. The primary libido of Rogozhin is, however, spurred on, precisely by her erotic coldness, to a mad desire for conquest and to an equally mad resentment because of her coldness. His erotic lust gradually passes into the lust for murder—a mood which hovers over his love like a cloud, until the crime actually takes place. The mysterious bond between the destroyer and his potential victim is at the root of the attraction between Nastasya and Rogozhin. Hence its undercurrent of horror. But Nastasya is so much under the spell of horror that even Myshkin's understanding devotion cannot save her. She is a plaything of her own obsession, as Rogozhin is of his. The meeting of the two is like the collision of two natural forces—a collision which makes a catastrophe inevitable.

A different dilemma is presented by Aglaya. Her capricious charm, so abundant in escapades, is the charm of a minx-like schoolgirl who is on the threshold of womanhood, but is still afraid of its mystery. It may be her fear of sex rather than real erotic love that draws her to Myshkin. She does not see a man in him, but what she regards as a noble human being. 'I ought to tell you that I never in my life met a man anything like him for noble simplicity of mind and for boundless trustfulness,' she says of him. 'I guessed that any one who liked could deceive him; and it was for this that I grew to love him.' At the same time she has that pride in chastity which Nastasya must have known before her adventure with Totsky. As though suspecting this, it is her own former 'perfection' (and not Aglaya's) that Nastasya admires in her letters to her rival, whom she urges to marry Prince Myshkin.

If in Nastasya sex has been killed by disgust, in Aglaya

it is not yet fully awakened. It comes into her love only in a roundabout way: through jealousy. Also in Myshkin's attitude towards her one can see a few flashes of awakening eroticism, but here we are left as much in the dark as are Aglaya's parents. If he was organically incapable (through his illness) of being a husband, then his wavering between Aglaya and Nastasya becomes less surprising. In both cases he is a 'brother' rather than a lover. One is inclined to agree with one of the characters who reproaches him: 'The most probable explanation of the matter is that you have never loved either the one or the other.' In spite of that, his and the two women's fate is the outcome of his indecision. And the outcome is tragic enough for all three.

IV

As for the secondary characters, Aglaya's mother, Lizaveta Prokofyevna, is arresting. She is an aged Aglaya: brusque, generous, inwardly noble, often very blunt, and with all that a grown-up child. This last feature makes her take the more readily to Myshkin. Ganya Ivolgin is the very embodiment of an ambitious mediocrity, with enough intelligence to realize how mediocre he really is. His father, the degraded General Ivolgin, can be regarded as the most perfect instance of a pathologic liar. The urge to lie is as much a need with him as alcohol is with a drunkard. Lebedyev is a crafty plebeian—somewhere on the margin between the lower and the middle strata. Belonging to no class and to no definite traditions, he is a grotesque 'intermediary', a mosaic of incongruous features, held together by his innate buffoonery. Frankly malicious are, however, Dostoevsky's portraits of the young nihilists one of whom, the consumptive Ippolit Terentyev, is a 'rebel'—vain and hysterical, but with a tragic touch.

The episode of Ippolit's confession (before his attempt at suicide) is one of Dostoevsky's favourite interpolations.

It connects, philosophically speaking, the ideas of Raskolnikov in *Crime and Punishment* with those of Kirillov in *The Possessed*. Ippolit is at the same time the spiritual contrast and antagonist of Myshkin. His rancour and self-assertion are those of a precocious boy who has been maltreated by life and is thus compelled to suppress not only his ambitions, but also his hidden generosity.

Such is the chaotic material which Dostoevsky's genius welded into a literary masterpiece.

VIII

STAVROGIN'S FATE

I

IN December 1869 Dostoevsky wrote to his friend, the poet Apollon Maikov, that he had conceived a 'tremendous novel' under the title, *Atheism*. On March 24th, 1870, he communicated some further particulars about his plan to Strakhov. Instead of one novel, he now intended to make five narratives, united by one and the same idea, and their general title was to be *The Life of a Great Sinner*. Dostoevsky never wrote the series. The drafts left by him prove, however, that a number of his projected themes and problems were included in his last three novels: *The Possessed*, *A Raw Youth*, and *The Brothers Karamazov*.

The most outspoken of them is *The Possessed*. It is also the most topical, at least in so far as Dostoevsky tried to penetrate into the inner essence of that revolutionary movement of the 'sixties which was steered by a group of active 'nihilists'. One should bear in mind that immediately after the abolition of serfdom, Russia was full of hopes and activities. Soon, however, reaction began to stir its ugly head once again. The awakened energies either turned into opposition, or else were driven underground where they assumed an ominous destructive character. The extreme left wing of the intelligentsia was particularly resentful. These 'nihilists', as they were called, combined quite comfortably, say, Buechner's philosophic materialism with all sorts of socialist schemes and Utopias. Their chief aim was, however, to destroy and to clear the ground for something better to come. It was not only their destructive fury, but also their schemes for 'something better' that Dostoevsky tried to debunk in his embittered novel. But in doing this he also exposed, through his very psychology, the deeper metaphysical roots of the Russian nihilism.

The first full-size portrait of a nihilist in Russian literature was Bazarov—the hero of Turgenev's *Fathers and Children* (1861). But while drawing that portrait, Turgenev incidentally indicated also the gulf, dividing the sentimental liberals of the 'forties from the reckless and aggressive positivists of the 'sixties. In *The Possessed* Dostoevsky gave his own version of the same theme. But instead of treating it with the detachment of his great contemporary, he permeated it with boundless anger, passion and even fear. His aim was to show the ultimate dangers—whether spiritual or social—of the Bazarov mentality. Or rather of the Belinsky-Herzen-Bakunin trend, to which he was so antagonistic. Moreover, he modelled a number of characters on actual people. Stavrogin, one of the principal figures, is supposed to be a composite portrait, suggested by the famous revolutionary and Marx's rival, Michael Bakunin, and by Speshnyov (from the days of the Petrashevsky circle).

As far as Bakunin is concerned, Dostoevsky saw and heard him on September 9th, 1867, in Geneva, during the congress of the international League of Peace and Freedom. The discussions he had witnessed at the congress must have stirred up in him quite a number of ideas, later embodied in his novel. These he probably interspersed with reminiscences of the Petrashevsky group. The Soviet critic Leonid Grossman even thinks that it was during the congress itself that Dostoevsky made the plan of the novel: with Stavrogin-Bakunin as its central hero. This conjecture carries less weight, however, if we consider the fact that Stavrogin appears on the stage when the plot of the novel is already far advanced.

Another character, Stavrogin's 'ape', Peter Verkhovensky, was suggested by the once notorious nihilist,

Nechayev. Even the plot of the novel was based on the activities of the Nechayev group, the behind-the-scenes of which were revealed by one of the most sensational trials of the 'sixties. The murder of Shatov in the novel refers to an actual crime, the victim of which was a certain student Ivanov (a former member of the Nechayev group). Verkhovensky's father, Stepan Trofimovitch—that pathetic mixture of a child, a sentimental fool, and a *schoene Seele*, was partly modelled on Professor Granovsky: a well-known liberal of the 'forties. And in the author Karmazinov Dostoevsky lampooned, with undisguised cruelty, his own rival Turgenev, whose faith in Western Europe irritated him even more than their personal differences.

II

Among the characters in *The Possessed*, Stavrogin strikes one as unfinished—a defect due largely to the editor Katkov, who left out the whole of Stavrogin's Confession. In spite of its vital significance, Dostoevsky too deleted Stavrogin's Confession in the later editions, thus leaving Stavrogin himself in the shape of a torso. But even had no cuts been made, Stavrogin would still remain the most puzzling figure ever created by the author. He is a self-divided Russian Hamlet, a new Raskolnikov, but on a larger and potentially more tragic scale. While Raskolnikov was a weak man crushed by a 'strong' idea, Stavrogin is a truly strong man, but unable to find an adequate channel for his strength. His boundless will-power is sapped at its roots by scepticism, by a lack of values and direction. As Kirillov says of him in his mentally stuttering manner: 'When he believes he does not believe that he believes, and when he does not believe, he does not believe that he does not believe.'

If we look at Stavrogin in the light of the preserved drafts for the novel, it becomes clear that Dostoevsky wanted to embody in him, apart from some further aspects of Raskolnikov's dilemma, the consequences of that 'atheism' which begins with the uprootedness from one's own nation (like the Russian intellectuals), and ends with the cosmic uprootedness of man. Unable to believe in overpersonal aims and values, the individual becomes not only self-centred, but also self-indulgent. This state is the more dangerous the more actual or potential strength there is in him. The process of inner disintegration, hastened on by his own inner wealth and strength —such is the tragedy of Stavrogin.

Being the most uprooted of all Dostoevsky's characters, Stavrogin is acutely aware of the emptiness of a world devoid of God, that is, of a higher meaning and Value. He cannot even protest, for he knows that a protest against irresponsible blind forces would be senseless. Existence becomes a cruel idiotic farce. And so all that remains to Stavrogin is to run away from the void and to waste his strength on trifles, on wanton ennui, on self-indulgence. From his 'Confession' we learn that at a moment of such ennui he had raped a little girl who afterwards committed suicide. Having discarded all moral values, he was at first callous about this crime. But after the girl's suicide he, too, felt—like Raskolnikov—a strange reaction: a need to confess and to *inflict punishment upon himself*.

'About that time, altogether for no definite reason, I took it into my head to cripple my life, but only in as disgusting a way as possible,' he says in his Confession. 'Already for about a year I had been thinking of shooting myself; but something better presented itself. One day, as I looked at the lame Marya Timofeyevna Lebyadkina, I suddenly determined to marry her. The idea of the marriage of Stavrogin to that lowest of creatures excited my nerves. Anything more monstrous it was impossible to imagine.'

While this craving for self-castigation made him indulge in some of his silliest exploits, his crime followed him like a shadow. It even pursued him in the shape of hallucinations. 'But it was intolerable to me, that image of her standing on the threshold with her raised and threatening little fist, merely that vision of her then, that moment "then", that shaking of her head. It is precisely that which I cannot endure, because since then it has come to me almost every day. Not that it comes itself, but that I bring it before myself and cannot help bringing it, although I can't live with it. . . . I know I can dismiss the thought of Matryosha even now whenever I want to. I am as completely master of my own will as ever. But the whole point is that I never wanted to do it. I myself do not want it and never shall.' This passage becomes clearer when he explains to Father Tikhon his intention to make public the confession of his own crime. 'I want to forgive myself, and that is my object, my whole object. Then only, I know, that vision will disappear. That is why I seek boundless suffering. I seek it myself.'

This inner craving for punishment is even more persistent in Stavrogin than in Raskolnikov. But true repentance is equally inaccessible to him. And like Raskolnikov he, too, despises all those who will or who might witness his self-castigation. As Father Tikhon remarks: 'You, it seems, already hate and despise before-hand all those who will read what is written here, and you challenge them.' The truth is that Stavrogin is much too conceited to demand or even to bear their pity. He prefers their anger.

Had the chapters under the heading 'Stavrogin's Con-fession', been included in the novel, the figure of Stavrogin would be clearer. When he appears in the novel, he is already a collection of 'doubles' whose context does not even disturb him any longer—he is past that stage. Equally conspicuous is Stavrogin's indifference to every-body and everything, which is a clear sign of his spiritual tedium: the tedium of non-being. Lack of all faith has ravaged his mind to such an extent that nothing on earth seems real to him. And so he himself ceases to be real and moves about like a sleep-walker or a phantom. Yet there is a magic in him. Like Myshkin, he too seems to be a medium of forces over which his consciousness has no control. But in Stavrogin's case these forces are of a negative 'infernal' kind. And they interest him only in so far as he can use them for his futile experiments upon other people's minds and wills. A number of men and women succumb to his elusive charm. Verkhovensky even dreams of him as a future dictator. But whereas people like Verkhovensky, Kirillov, and Shatov passionately cling to some of his single ideas, he himself sees in them only self-deceptions—too weak to make him escape from himself.

III

In the order of Stavrogin's self-deceptions (mentioned retrospectively), sensual indulgence came first. In this he resembles Svidrigailov. Stavrogin's 'Confession' might have been written by him. But the wildest sensual experiments only increased Stavrogin's ennui. He felt neither pleasure nor remorse. Even his clandestine marriage to the half-witted cripple, Marya Timofeyevna, proved of no avail.

'Is it true that when you were in Petersburg you belonged to a secret society for practising beastly sensuality?' Shatov—his one-time follower—shouts at him during one of their meetings. 'Is it true that you could give lessons to the Marquis de Sade? Is it true that you decoyed and corrupted children? Is it true that you declared you saw no distinction in beauty between some brutal obscene action and any great exploit, even the sacrifice of life for the good of humanity? . . . I don't know either why evil is hateful and good is beautiful, but I know why the sense of that distinction is effaced and lost in people like Stavrogins! . . . Do you know why you made that base and shameful marriage? Simply because the shame and senselessness of it reached a pitch of genius! You married from a passion for martyrdom, from a craving for remorse, through moral sensuality. It was a lacerating of the nerves. Defiance of common sense was too tempting. Stavrogin and a wretched half-witted, crippled beggar!'

'You are a psychologist,' said Stavrogin, turning paler and paler, 'though you are partly mistaken as to the reason of my marriage.'

Stavrogin's deleted confession proves that Shatov *was* 'partly mistaken'. The deepest reasons why Stavrogin drugged himself with vice were hidden from him. So was perhaps the fact that he had gone after the flesh with such frenzy precisely because he was a voluptuary without real passion. 'I have tried the depths of debauchery and wasted my strength over it. But I don't like vice, and I don't want it,' he says in his last letter. His relations with women in the novel make one even suspect that—like his supposed prototype Bakunin—he was undersexed. His behaviour towards Liza, as well as hers towards him (after the night they had spent together) can be explained only through the assumption that he was impotent. This, by the way, would shed some further light upon his excursions into sadism.

It was for similar reasons that Stavrogin took up revolutionary activities. He mingled with the fanatical nihilists, with the 'possessed', as though hoping he might become infected by their own obsession and thus find a temporary shelter from himself. He tried on them some of his own ideas. But even the ardour of Shatov and Kirillov (followers of his two simultaneous yet utterly opposed doctrines) was of no use to him. What to others seemed a revelation, was to him but 'old commonplace, the same from the beginning of time'. Here is one of the reproaches Shatov hurls at him:

'It was a teacher uttering weighty words and a pupil who was raised from the dead. Perhaps during those very days you were infecting the heart of that hapless creature, that maniac Kirillov, with poison. . . . You confirmed malignant ideas in him, and brought him to the verge of insanity.'

'I was not deceiving either of you. I was not deceiving you then; in persuading you I was perhaps more concerned with myself than with you,' Stavrogin said enigmatically.

Shatov then enumerates, in a passionate tirade, some of those ideas with which Stavrogin had once kindled a new life in him. But Stavrogin answers with the same indifference as before:

'I assure you that I should be very glad to confirm all that you said just now, every syllable of it, but——'

'But you want a hare? . . . your own nasty expression.' Shatov laughed spitefully. 'To cook your hare you must first catch it; to believe in God you must first have a God.'

'Tell me, have you caught your hare?'

'Don't dare to ask me in such words! Ask differently!'

'Certainly, I'll ask you differently. I only want to know do you believe in God yourself?'

'I believe in Russia. . . . I believe in her orthodoxy. . . . I believe that the new advent will take place in Russia. . . . I believe——'

'And in God? In God?'

'I—I *will* believe in God.'

Thus, in a few words, each of them reveals his secret. Stavrogin has already gone through all his deceptions, while the God-seeker Shatov is still clutching to his, lest he fall into the same void which has engulfed his former teacher.

IV

Like Myshkin in *The Idiot*, Stavrogin too remains static to the end. And in the same way people and events revolve around him, although he does not want it. The ideas which once emanated from him, seem to have acquired in his followers an independent life of their own.

Like the microbes in Raskolnikov's dream, they infect those around him and turn them into maniacs. Stavrogin is the only one who remains cold and indifferent. But he loathes his own indifference. 'Do you know that I looked upon our iconoclasts with spite, from envy of their hopes,' he wrote to Darya. 'But you have no need to be afraid. I could not be of them, for I never shared anything with them. And to do it for fun, from spite, I could not either, not because I am afraid of the ridiculous—I cannot be afraid of the ridiculous—but because I have, after all, the habits of a gentleman, and it disgusted me. But if I had felt more spite and envy of them, I might perhaps have joined them.'

Even his last refuge—strength for strength's sake—fails him. He maintains a superhuman composure when Shatov insults him publicly. He calmly acknowledges his 'shameful marriage', faces Gaganov's pistol with insulting boredom; yet far from intoxicating him, his 'immense power' once more turns against him, since he is unable to give it a creative direction.

'I have tried my strength everywhere,' he writes before his end. 'As long as I was experimenting for myself and for others it seemed infinite, as it has all my life. But to what to apply my strength, that is what I have never seen, and do not see now. My desires are too weak; they are not enough to guide me.' And again, 'One may argue about everything endlessly, but from me nothing has come but negation, with no greatness of soul, no force. Even negation has not come from me. Everything has always been petty and spiritless.' Like Svidrigailov, he makes a final attempt to escape from his own fate by means of a woman. He hopes for a love so strong and beautiful that it could 'at last set up some aim' for him. But from Liza (who has run away from her fiancé to Stavrogin) we learn that, instead of the expected miracle, there was only a new deception—on both sides.

'I knew I did not love you, and I ruined you,' Stavrogin

complains after the night they had spent together. 'Yes, I accepted the moment for my own; I had a hope. . . . I've had it for a long time . . . my last hope. . . . I could not resist the radiance that flooded my heart when you came in to me yesterday of yourself, alone, of your own accord. I suddenly believed . . . perhaps I have faith in it still. . . .'

'I won't be your nurse,' Liza cuts him short, 'although of course, you need one as much as any crippled creature. I always fancied that you would take me to some place where there was a huge wicked spider, big as a man, and we should spend our lives looking at it and being afraid of it. That's how our love would spend itself.'

His inner vacuum, the vacuum of non-being, is the only thing that does not deceive him like all the rest, including the idea of suicide. 'I know I ought to kill myself, to brush myself off the earth like a nasty insect; but I am afraid of showing greatness of soul. I know that it will be another shame again—the last deception in an endless series of deceptions,' he writes in his letter. For a while he intends to escape with Darya, the woman who still loves him, and vegetate with her in the canton Uri in Switzerland where he had bought a house. 'It is a very dull place, a narrow valley, the mountains restrict both vision and thought. It's very gloomy.' But in the end he prefers a quicker death. He 'brushes himself off the earth like a nasty insect'.

Judging by his drafts, Dostoevsky must have thought for a while of Stavrogin's regeneration. The chapters dealing with Stavrogin's confession and his talk with Father Tikhon unmistakably point to such a possibility. But while working out the novel, the author altered his plan. This was the reason why he omitted those chapters also in later editions. He preferred to stress the inner blind-alley that lay in store for the uprooted radicals and the over-Europeanized nobles. While still thinking of Stavrogin's rebirth, Dostoevsky made him say (in a draft):

'Even before I rejected and hated nihilism, but now I see that worst of all and most guilty of all are we aristocrats, who are uprooted from the soil, and it is precisely we who must be reborn first and not the others; we are the greatest rottenness, all the curse lies upon us and comes from us.'

The question which follows and links up this dilemma of Stavrogin with that of Shatov, is whether such an intellectual ever can sincerely return to the soil, to the people, and through the people's faith to religion and Christianity which 'alone can bring man back to the spring of living water and save him from decay'. But in the case of Shatov we see only a passionate will to return to faith and God. He is unable to go beyond a mere will to believe, although he knows that the alternative is Stavrogin's impasse. And Shatov is a commoner, a man of the people, while the other revolutionaries in the novel are nobles, devoid of any contact either with the soil or with the people. Consequently they can only destroy, until they themselves are destroyed.

V

If regarded from this angle, *The Possessed* would almost seem a novel *à thèse*, touching upon one of Russia's most topical dilemmas of that period: the relationship between the intelligentsia and the people. But this is done only indirectly. What the author is here concerned with are the ultimate spiritual issues, illustrated by Stavrogin's conflicting 'idea-forces'. These, once let loose, become actual obsessions with such intellectuals as Kirillov, Shatov and Verkhovensky. At the same time they are also Stavrogin's 'doubles', as it were, arising out of his disintegrating consciousness.

Kirillov is a man with a tremendous religious thirst and temperament who had lost all religious convictions. So he embraced with all the greater fervour Stavrogin's idea of the superman or man-God as a kind of substitute. But the idea, much too strong for him, crushed him at the very moment when he revelled in it with ecstasy. Kirillov brought Raskolnikov's self-will to its final conclusions and actually turned it into a new religion, or anti-religion, to which he sacrificed everything, including himself. The starting-point of his creed is: 'If God exists, all is His will and from His will I cannot escape. If not, it is all my will, and I am bound to show self-will. Because all will has become mine.' Acting on this principle, the atheist Kirillov shows his self-will more radically than Raskolnikov. Instead of killing another human being, he kills himself—also for the sake of a 'principle'. Unable to find any sense or value in an existence which is but a play of blind forces, a 'vaudeville of the devils', his consciousness refuses to accept such a world. And since he cannot destroy the world, he destroys himself. For him suicide is the only logical outcome of what might be called religious atheism. It is also the climax of his protest and self-will. 'Can it be that no one in the whole planet, after making an end of God and believing in his own will, will dare to express his self-will on the most vital point? I may be the only one, but I'll do it. I am bound to shoot myself by my own hands. . . .' The final logical and psychological act of his self-will is self-destruction.

As for Verkhovensky, he is too shallow to care for anything except destruction, but this becomes a mania with him. In Kirillov is shown by the author the inner connexion between atheism and suicide; in Verkhovensky —between atheism and a merely destructive revolution. Verkhovensky's nihilism is no longer an expression of the negative lust for power, nor is it a protest. It is not only anti-religious, but also (and this is the paradox) anti-revolutionary, as we can see from Shigalyov's scheme for compulsory 'happiness' on earth. Shigalyov starts with unlimited freedom, but ends—and inevitably so— with unlimited despotism over a humanity of standardized robots after the Nazi pattern. Verkhovensky wants to pave the way to it through destruction for its own sake.

'Listen,' he raves in his talk with Stavrogin, 'first of all we'll make an upheaval. We shall penetrate to the peasantry. On all sides we see vanity puffed up out of all proportions, brutal, monstrous appetites. . . . Do you know how many we shall catch by little ready-made ideas? The Russian God has already been vanquished by cheap vodka. Oh, this generation has only to grow up. One or two generations of vice are essential now; monstrous, abject vice by which a man is transformed into a loathsome, cruel, egoistic reptile. That's what we need. And what's more, a little "fresh blood" that we may get accustomed to it. . . . We will proclaim destruction. . . . We'll set legends going. . . . There's going to be such an upset as the world has never seen before. . . . Russia will be overwhelmed by darkness, the earth will weep for its old gods.'

VI

The virulence of this novel is due to the fact that Dostoevsky put into it too much of his own personal animosity which he was unable to sublimate to the end.[1] This may account for some of its technical drawbacks, especially for its lack of a definite central hero. The first portion of the novel is dominated by Stepan Trofimovich. Stavrogin enters late, while Peter Verkhovensky is worked out so much in one single direction that he is more convincing as a 'possessed' than as a human being. There is in it also a certain wavering (especially in the second half) between the narrative in the first person and the agitated *reportage*.

More compact, on the whole, is the ideological structure. There is great subtlety in the contrast and the affinity between the 'liberal' generation of the 'forties and their nihilist descendants, from whom the parents

[1] Shatov voices some of the 'converted' Dostoevsky's own ideas about Russia, Orthodoxy and religion.

turn away with horror. Yet as shown by Dostoevsky, the destructive radicalism was a child of the former senti-mental rationalists and liberals. Anyhow, *The Possessed* is a reduction *ad absurdum* of the irreligious kind of individualism, carried to its farthest logical as well as psychological conclusions. Stavrogin represents its tragic blind-alley; Shatov—a panicky quest for a religious outlet; Kirillov—the destructive solipsism; and Verkhovensky— the social chaos in the style of Raskolnikov's dream in Siberia. As there is no deeper irrational tie between men on the one hand, and between mankind and the Universe on the other, everybody becomes self-centred, an end unto himself. But the human *ego* begins to disintegrate through its very self-centredness; or else submits to the greatest tyranny (of persons, ideas, or even vices) rather than endure 'freedom' for its own sake.

This book—so reactionary on the surface—is a biting satire only against those pseudo-revolutionaries, whom Shatov stigmatizes as 'the enemies of all true life, out-of-date liberals who are afraid of their own independence, the flunkeys of thought, the enemies of individuality and freedom, the decrepit advocates of deadness and rotten-ness. All they have to offer is senility, a glorious medio-crity of the most bourgeois kind, contemptible shallow-ness, a jealous equality, equality without individual dignity, equality as it is understood by flunkeys.'

It was revolutionaries of this kind that Dostoevsky attacked in *The Possessed*. And in the background of it all there looms the eternal problem of personality, of culture, of God. Of God in particular. The nihilist Verkhovensky relates jestingly to Stavrogin how 'a grizzled old stager' of a captain had listened to a discussion upon atheism, then suddenly stood up in the middle of the room and exclaimed, as though talking to himself: 'If there is no God, how can I be a captain, then?'

'I didn't understand it,' says Verkhovensky, 'I meant to ask you about it.'

'He expressed a rather sensible idea,' answers the atheist Stavrogin.

The Possessed is a further development of the main theme indicated in *The Notes from the Underworld* and in *Crime and Punishment*. When the first of these two works appeared, Dostoevsky complained in a letter to his brother that the stupid censorship had cut out all his ideas about the need of returning to Christ and to religion. *The Possessed* stresses such a need more categorically than any of his previous novels. Towards the end, the dying Stepan Trofimovitch even compares the nihilists with the devils exorcized by Christ, and hopes that the same miracle will happen to Russia. 'And all the devils will come forth, all impurity, all rottenness that was putrefying on the surface . . . and they will beg of themselves to enter into swine. . . . But the sick man will be healed and will sit at the feet of Jesus, and all will look at him with astonishment.'

New variations of these motives can be studied in Dostoevsky's last two novels, *A Raw Youth* and *The Brothers Karamazov*.

IX

A RAW YOUTH

I

AMONG Dostoevsky's five great novels, *A Raw Youth* stands somewhat apart. It is his only important work in which the external causation (including various detective and gangster tricks) prevails, even to the detriment of its excellent psychological pages. One is aware in it also of a certain wavering between several theses and ideas, which either are not worked out or else are soon dropped by the author—like the idea of power at the beginning of the novel. The narrative centres round what Dostoevsky calls an 'accidental' Russian family, or at least round two of its members. One of them is the former serf-owner and now an impoverished aristocrat, Versilov; and the other, his illegitimate son Arkady whose mother had been a serf in Versilov's household.

It is possible that Dostoevsky wanted to put a topical meaning into such a union. After the reforms of 1861 the mixing of the hitherto separated classes became inevitable. The problem of bridging over the gulf between the cultured upper layer and the 'people' arose in all its acuteness. This novel is largely a history of the *liaison* between an aristocrat and a woman of the people. On the surface there is little in common between the two persons coming from such different strata. The union itself is illegitimate. So is its offspring Arkady, who is hardly even acknowledged by his own father. Yet Arkady combines features of both classes: the 'inferiority complex' and the broadness of the people, the mental alertness as well as the cultural instincts of Versilov. He is in a state of fermentation—rather chaotic, but full of vitality and promise. His obvious task is to harmonize his contrasts and also to achieve an adjustment with his father—such as would make even the union between his two parents deeper, less 'accidental' than before.

It is a difficult task. The more so because Dostoevsky depicts Arkady's transition from 'the raw youth' period to early manhood. He has also chosen the most suitable method for dealing with such a transition: the form of personal reminiscences on the part of Arkady himself. The narrative is often confused and garrulous. The reader's patience is tried by sentences such as 'but more of this later', 'to avoid muddle I will anticipate the order of events'. And as for the external intricacies of the plot, they accumulate, particularly towards the end, past all belief. In spite of that, the novel is a remarkable psychological and (to some extent) even social document.

II

The action of *A Raw Youth* takes place in Petersburg at a time when Russia was undergoing rapid external and inner changes. One can feel in the novel the breaking-up of the old forms of life, and also that mixture of classes and conditions which—after centuries of serfdom—heralded a capitalist 'bourgeois' age. Like everywhere else, capitalism in Russia fostered some of the worst plutocratic and plebeian (as distinct from democratic) tendencies. Here its orgy threatened to become even more unpalatable than in Western Europe, since Russia had weaker cultural traditions to counteract it. Dostoevsky with his peculiar populist trend, could not help looking upon all that with apprehension. 'The present day is the golden age of mediocrity and callousness, of passion for ignorance, idleness, inefficiency, a craving for everything ready-made', one of his characters complains. 'No one thinks; it's rare for any one to work out an idea for himself.' And in the epilogue we read this remark: 'Something is happening to us to-day and in the recent past. It is not that the worthless attach themselves to the highest stratum of society, but, on the contrary, with light-hearted haste, fragments are torn from what is fine and noble and thrown into one mass with the lawless and the envious.'

As in most of his works, the author introduces us to a pageantry of men belonging to several social strata: decaying aristocrats (Prince Sergey, the old Prince Sokolsky, and Versilov himself), representatives of the people, revolutionaries, *déclassés*, and the new 'practical' business men (Stebelkov). On the other hand, *A Raw Youth* testifies to Dostoevsky's wish to correct some of his former views and ideas. His attitude towards revolutionaries, for example, is less condemning this time than in *The Possessed*. He also shows a greater tolerance with regard to the Russian liberals and self-exiled 'wanderers abroad' of Herzen's type. In Versilov's dream of the golden age (taken over from Stavrogin's 'Confession') he even conjures up a vision of mankind's future which is a complete antithesis of Shigalyov's 'system' in *The Possessed*, although it is based on the same philosophic premise. As the novel appeared in the liberal *Fatherland's Annals*, edited by Nekrasov and Saltykov, such a change, after the 'reactionary' fury in his previous novel, might easily seem a compromise with the editors. The change had, however, more substantial reasons as one can gather both from Dostoevsky's correspondence and *The Journal of an Author* of that period.

As a novel this work is difficult to classify. It resembles the type of the *Bildungsroman*, at least in so far as it unfolds the inner growth and changes in a youth during his formative period. But in contrast to Goethe's harmonious *Wilhelm Meister* or Gottfried Keller's wistfully idyllic *Der Gruene Heinrich*, *A Raw Youth* is in a dynamic agitation. It describes a short period only: about a year, during which Arkady makes his decisive steps towards a mature life. And since that period involves, above all, certain changes in Arkady's relations with Versilov, the novel marks a sublimation of the friction between them.

III

But for a few early glimpses, Arkady meets his father only at the age of twenty, although he has been longing for his affection since childhood. And his childhood was none too pleasant. As a child of an 'accidental' family, he had been despised and even maltreated by his comrades in a Moscow boarding-school. The result was a feeling of inferiority, morbid self-consciousness, and that keen gift of observation which comes from self-defence. At the same time Versilov's indifference to him as a child had filled his little soul with rancour which was all the stronger because he secretly admired him. The longing to establish a true affection between his father and himself gradually became a part of his inner life. Such an affection now actually grew up between the two and, in the end, influenced their immediate destinies.

In spite of his reserve, Arkady is too young and too impulsive to hide his ideas or emotions. He carries his heart on his sleeve. Not so his father. Versilov is rarely without a mask, or several masks, especially before Arkady. It takes quite a time before we begin to distinguish his real face, which is of a highly complicated nature. He combines certain features of Stavrogin with those of Myshkin. Even his wavering between Katerina Ivanovna (the type of Dostoevsky's 'fatal' woman) and Arkady's meek, self-sacrificing mother is reminiscent of Myshkin's indecision between Aglaya and Nastasya. His duality and scepticism bring him, however, near to Stavrogin, from whose fate he is saved partly by his fastidiousness, and partly by his ceaseless quest. For with all his scepticism he is a God-seeker. One of the characters describes him as a 'very proud man, and many very proud people like to believe in God, especially those who despise other people. Many strong natures seem to have a natural craving to find some one or something to which they can do homage. Strong natures often find it very difficult

to bear the burden of their strength. . . . They turn to
God to avoid doing homage to men, of course without
recognizing how it comes about in them: to do homage
to God is not so humiliating. They become the most
fervent believers—or, to be more accurate, the most
fervently desirous of believing; but they take this desire
for belief itself. These are the people who most frequently
become disillusioned in the end.'

Versilov's weakness and frequent irresponsibility are
due to his disintegration rather than to absence of strength.
In this, too, he resembles Stavrogin. And like Stavrogin,
he exercises an uncanny fascination upon a number of
people. Arkady is positively infatuated with his personality, even though he hates him at times. Versilov
guesses his son's feelings, yet his natural delicacy prevents
him from showing his awakened paternal interest and
tenderness. His restraint leads to a rude outburst on
Arkady's part. The resentful 'raw youth' leaves his
mother's (and Versilov's) flat where he has been staying
since his arrival from Moscow, and settles down on his
own. Versilov understands the reason of Arkady's temper
and comes to see him after the quarrel. The two have a
hearty talk. Arkady is overjoyed.

' "I knew you'd be sure to come," he remarks when
seeing Versilov off.

' "And I knew that you knew I should be sure to come.
Thank you, my dear."

'He was silent. We had reached the outer door, and
I still followed him. He opened the door; the wind
rushing in blew out my candle. Then I clutched his
hand. It was pitch dark. He started but said nothing.
I stopped over his hand and kissed it greedily several
times, many times.

' "My darling boy, why do you love me so much?" he
said, but in quite a different voice. His voice quivered,
there was a ring of something new in it as though it were
not he who spoke.

'I tried to answer something, but couldn't, and ran upstairs. I slipped by the landlord and went into my room, fastened the latch, and without lighting the candle threw myself on my bed, buried my face in the pillow, and cried.'

Then he adds rather ominously: 'But didn't I make him suffer for it? I became frightfully overbearing. There was no reference to this scene between us afterwards.'

Nevertheless the ice was broken. The process of adjustment began on both sides. But it had to pass through a number of vagaries before it was completed.

IV

One of such vagaries is Arkady's episode with Katerina Ivanovna, who once had stood very close to Versilov. Versilov still loves her secretly, and with that passion in which love is hardly distinguishable from hatred. Arkady says of him later: 'If she (Katerina) were to marry him, he would spurn her from him the day after the wedding. For such a wild outrageous love is like a fit, like a deadly noose, like an illness, and—as soon as it is gratified—the scales fall from the eyes at once and the opposite feeling comes—loathing and hatred, the desire to strangle, to crush!'

When Katerina Ivanovna appears, Arkady falls in love with her at once. She is his first great and pure love. Never before has he been so near to his father as when he talks to him, with youthful glee (and without knowing Versilov's secret), of his love for Katerina who has just become engaged to a rather conventional baron. Versilov, however, takes advantage of Arkady's confidence for his own purpose. His 'second self' is aroused to such a pitch of love-hatred which would be almost unthinkable in a normal being. What he really wants is to destroy—from jealousy—Katerina's engagement. And in the end he succeeds. In the meantime Katerina is anxious to get hold of a letter which might compromise her in the eyes of her old father and prejudice her expected fortune. By a caprice of fate the letter is in the hands of Arkady. But instead of destroying it or giving it to Katerina, he keeps it without any reason. This letter soon becomes a hectic affair: everybody and everything begins to circle round it. An intricate plot is concocted behind Arkady's back to snatch the letter from him. A number of people take part in the intrigue: some of them hoping to get hold of Katerina's fortune, others to blackmail her, others to save her. The climax is reminiscent of a Hollywood gangster-film.

Fortunately, the psychology of Arkady and Versilov provides a compensation. With each chapter Arkady's experiences become more involved and chaotic. He mixes with aristocrats, gamblers, blackguards. He drinks, tries his luck at the roulette-table, is insulted in a gambling den —in short, he burns the candle at both ends, until he is on the verge of a moral and physical breakdown. His adventures are often pathetically muddled and crowded with contrasts, as is to be expected of a 'raw youth' of twenty. Yet one is aware all the time that the material out of which he is made is good and that he will crystallize into something worth while.

A steadying process begins for him only after several catastrophic incidents, including a dangerous illness. The most beneficent influence he undergoes during that phase is, however, the one exercised by his mother's aged husband, Makar Ivanovitch. This Russian peasant, whom Dostoevsky describes in an almost hagiographic vein, turns up from his peregrinations during Arkady's most critical days, and dies shortly after. His serenity, kindness, and wisdom bring peace to all. And his death marks the actual turning point in the lives of Arkady and Versilov. The long talk between father and son, after Makar's death, is perhaps the most revealing portion of the novel. Sincere, tender, yet full of a delicate reserve, the two become definitely adjusted to each other. Having established with his father the bond he was craving for, Arkady concludes his chaotic 'raw youth' period.

A change also comes over Versilov who is compelled to fight a last decisive battle with his 'second self', still madly in love with Katerina. In a moment of irresponsible exasperation he even intends to murder or at least to disgrace her. But an accident intervenes, and the storm is over. The end seems 'happy'. An atmosphere of serene resignation indicates a new life for Versilov and the members of his 'accidental' family.

V

Like Dostoevsky's other novels, *A Raw Youth* is teeming with ideas, typical of the author's own fermentation in the 'seventies. Versilov embodies many features and opinions of Dostoevsky himself. Through Arkady he even describes certain reminiscences of his own childhood. Also the satisfactory solution of Arkady's 'father-complex' may reflect perhaps occasional wishes of Dostoevsky the boy.

Dostoevsky's more generous attitude towards the liberal and revolutionary forces has been mentioned already. Even his cardinal idea—the idea of God and its effect upon humanity—was modified for a while. The hidden sceptic Versilov found an alternative to God not in man's self-will but in an intensified love for the world and mankind. Men deprived of God and left forlorn in the universe 'would begin to draw together more closely and more lovingly; they would clutch one another's hands, realizing that they were all that was left for one another! The great idea of immortality would have vanished, and they would have to fill its place; and all the wealth of love lavished of old upon Him, Who was immortal, would be turned upon the whole of nature, on the world, on men, on every blade of grass. They would inevitably grow to love the earth and life as they gradually became aware of their own transitory and finite nature.'

Also his views on Europe and Russia show an advance upon those expressed by Shatov with his exclusive 'Russian God'. Versilov voices the same kind of synthesis between Russia and Europe, between the Slavophils and the 'Westerners', which became so prominent in Dostoevsky during the last years of his life. He is particularly emphatic about the pan-humanity and the broad instinctive sympathy with all nations on the part of the Russian intellectual *élite*. 'Among Russians has been created by the ages a type of the highest culture, never seen before and existing nowhere else in the world—the type of world-wide compassion for all. . . . A Frenchman can serve not only his France, but humanity, only on condition that he remains French to the utmost possible degree, and it's the same for the Englishman and the German. Only to the Russian, even in our day, has been vouchsafed the capacity to become most of all Russian only when he is most European. That is the essential difference between us Russians and all the rest, and in that respect the position in Russia is as nowhere else. I am in France a Frenchman, with a German I am a German, with the ancient Greek I am a Greek, and by that very fact I am most typically Russian, and am most truly serving Russia, for I am bringing out her leading idea. . . . To the Russian, Europe is as precious as Russia: every stone in her is cherished and dear. Europe is as much our fatherland as Russia.'

This is how Dostoevsky linked up the history of an 'accidental' family with the broader universal problems and ideas, expressed in *The Brothers Karamazov*, and also in his Pushkin speech, delivered only a few months before his death.

X

'THE TWO KINDS OF TRUTH'

Ivan Karamazov

I

The Brothers Karamazov represents not only the apex of Dostoevsky's art and thought, but also his final vision of existence. His earliest jottings for this vast encyclo-paedia of Russian mentality go as far back as 1876, but he actually began writing it in 1878. As in *A Raw Youth*, Dostoevsky took up in this work, once more, a whole family. The scene of action is, however, not Peters-burg, but the provinces. The Karamazov family, whose destinies the author unfolds, is more varied and much more striking than the one in his previous novel. To begin with, the old Karamazov, although a dissolute representative of the former serf-owning class, is still full of vitality, of animal appetites and passions. Of his four sons Mitya is as chaotic and impulsive as his parent, but he is made of better material. Also the passion he indulges in is on a higher plane and actually becomes ennobled—both in him and in the woman he loves—by a sudden catastrophe. In Ivan all that energy has become an intellectual, and in Alyosha a spiritual force. Their illegitimate half-brother, the flunkey Smerdyakov, is, however, a mental and moral abortion.

The fate of this family is interlaced with a number of other people: the *pater Seraphicus* (Zosima) in the Monastery, the 'infernal' Grushenka, the hysterical Katerina, and the delightful crowd of little boys grouped around Alyosha. The inner causation of events is worked out with a greater mastery than in *A Raw Youth*. So are the changes in the characters. The axis of the plot is the rivalry between Mitya and his father for the favours of Grushenka, the murder of the old Karamazov forming the climax of the novel. Mitya is falsely accused and convicted, but he accepts the suffering and (in contrast to Raskolnikov) becomes a new human being. Smerdyakov, the actual murderer and a follower of Ivan's popularized 'all things are lawful', hangs himself. And Ivan, whose consciousness has to endure a final clash between the two opposite sets of values, collapses under the weight of his own cleavage.

As a complement to these 'human-all-too-human' goings on in the town, we find a less worldly atmosphere in the Monastery whose central figure is Father Zosima. The mediator between both worlds is the young Alyosha. He actually lives in the Monastery as a novice, but is given complete freedom of movement. The spiritual backbone of the novel is, however, the conflict (or rather the incompatibility) of the two truths and valuations of life: the truth of Ivan, and the truth of Zosima. It was through these two characters that Dostoevsky now voiced his own final secrets and ideas, transformed by his art.

II

Ivan Karamazov shares many features with Raskolnikov and Stavrogin. He represents a new aspect of the same dilemma. Raskolnikov fled in horror from the weight of 'beyond good and evil'. Stavrogin tried to forget it in futile experiments upon himself and others. Ivan Karamazov, however, is poised on that narrow ridge which separates the world of 'all things are lawful' from the possibility of Value. He passionately wishes to accept the latter, but is hampered all the time by his intellectual honesty—by the integrity of his own scepticism. In addition, Ivan is swayed by a consuming thirst for life, even if he is unable to find a meaning of life. It is precisely the abundance of his irrational vitality that keeps him alive, in spite of his destructive intellect. 'I have a longing for life and go on living *in spite of logic*,' he says to Alyosha.

'I have asked myself many times whether there is in the world any despair that would overcome this frantic and perhaps unseemly thirst for life in me, and I have come to the conclusion that there is not. Though I may not believe in the order of the universe, yet I love the sticky leaves as they open in spring. I love the blue sky. . . . It is not a matter of intellect or logic, it is loving with one's inside, one's stomach.'

This contest between his logic and his 'inside' is, however, less painful than the cleavage of his spirit with its contradictory impulses. Burning with the desire to sing hosanna, he is compelled to 'rebel'. Craving for life, he is yet forced to reject it. Unlike Stavrogin, Ivan admits the existence of God. Or at least he realizes the incompetence of our reason to deny it. But even while acknowledging God, he repudiates Him as devoid of Value. His outraged sense of justice cannot reconcile the universal suffering, the beastliness of man, the evil and mockery of life with the conception of a wise and just God. It is his conscience that raises a wall between God and the Value. For Ivan (as for Dostoevsky) social justice is or ought to be but a part of the metaphysical problem of justice.

'Imagine that you are creating a fabric of human destiny with the object of making men happy in the end, giving them peace and rest at last, but that it was essential and inevitable to torture to death only one tiny creature—that baby beating its breast with its fist—and to found the edifice on its unavenged tears, would you consent to be the architect on those conditions?' he asks his brother Alyosha.

'No, I would not consent,' answers Alyosha.

'I say nothing of the suffering of the grown-up people. They have eaten their apple, damn them all! But the little ones! Without suffering, I am told, man could not have existed on earth, for he could not know good and evil. Why should he know that diabolical good and evil when it costs so much? The whole of knowledge is not worth a child's suffering. What comfort is it to me that there are none guilty and that cause follows effect simply and directly, and that I know it—I must have justice, or I will destroy myself. And not justice in some remote infinite time and space, but here on earth, and that I could see myself. I want to see it, and if I am dead by then, let me rise again, for if it happens without me it will be too unfair. Surely I haven't suffered simply that I, my crimes and sufferings, may manure the soil of the future harmony for somebody else. I want to see with my own eyes the hind lie down with the lion, and the victim rise up and embrace the murderer. I want to be there when every one suddenly understands what it has all been for.'

After referring to some incredible tortures perpetrated on the 'little ones',[1] Ivan raises the problem of their suffering simply because children are not guilty of any 'sins'. And as for the religious theories of retribution upon children, they shock him as something monstrous. 'If I must suffer for the eternal harmony, what have children to do with it? It's beyond all comprehension why they should suffer, and why they should pay for the harmony. Why should they too furnish material to enrich the soil for the harmony of the future? And if it is really true that they must share responsibility for their father's crimes, such a truth is not of this world and is beyond my comprehension.'

Ivan's moral sense cannot accept suffering on such terms. Even if some higher truth should eventually be revealed as a reward and compensation for it all, he would repudiate the truth itself. Such a truth is not worth the price already paid for it. Nor is the future 'harmony', provided such a thing be possible at all. 'I don't want harmony. From love of humanity I don't want it. I would rather be left with my unavenged suffering and unsatisfied indignation, *even if I were wrong.*

[1] Dostoevsky dealt with some of those criminal cases also in his *Journal of an Author.*

Besides, too high a price is asked for harmony; it is beyond
our means to pay so much to enter on it. And so I hasten
to give back my entrance ticket, and if I am an honest
man I am bound to give it back as soon as possible. And
that I am doing. It is not God that I don't accept, only
I most respectfully return Him the ticket.'[1]

III

This is, however, only one side of Ivan's dilemma. If
God exists, He is responsible for all the suffering and
injustice in a world created by Him. In this case God is
a supernatural Monster which must be rejected by a
highly developed conscience—until He has revealed His
'secret' and given a satisfactory account. For God is as
much responsible to man as man is responsible to God.
The alternative is that God does not exist at all. Which
means that no one is responsible for anything: the
world is but a 'vaudeville of devils', and 'all things are
lawful'—logically at least, if not actually.

Kirillov in *The Possessed* accepted this alternative and
made the necessary conclusions which led him to suicide.
Ivan's mind, however, wavers all the time between the
two contradictory possibilities, while his sense of justice
claims in vain for an outlet, for Value. This struggle
reaches its climax during Ivan's delirious talk with the
devil: a colossal figure in comparison with which even
Goethe's Mephistopheles looks like a naughty scamp who

---

[1] It may be of interest that the radical critic Belinsky, whose atheism
Dostoevsky detested, expressed the same idea in almost identical
terms. 'If I had the opportunity of climbing up to the highest rung
in the ladder of mankind's evolution,' he writes, 'even there I would
demand an account for all the victims of life and history: the victims
of chance, superstitution, Inquisition, Philip II, etc., etc. Otherwise
I would hurl myself down, headlong, from that highest rung. I refuse
happiness even as a gift, unless my mind is set at peace with regard
to my brothers by blood, bone of my bone, flesh of my flesh. One
says that harmony itself is conditioned by disharmony. This may
perhaps be gratifying for the lovers of music, but it certainly is not
for those who are doomed to express disharmony in their own
experience.'

has read Voltaire. The whole of that episode is the profoundest thing Dostoevsky ever wrote. What increases
its force is the tone of the devil who mockingly paraphrases
the European philosophy, laughing all the time at its
inconsistency.

'Is there a God or not?' shouts Ivan at him.

'My dear fellow,' the devil answers ironically, 'upon
my word I don't know. . . . I have the same philosophy
as you. *Je pense, donc je suis*. I know that for a fact; all
the rest, all these worlds, God and even Satan—all that
is not proved to my mind. Does all that exist of itself,
or is it only an emanation of myself.'

And as for the 'secret', all he can tell about it is this
whimsical tirade: 'Before time was, by some decree which
I could never make out, I was predestined to deny. And
yet I am genuinely good-hearted and not at all inclined
to negation. No, you must go and deny; without denial
there would be nothing but one "hosanna". But nothing
but hosanna is not enough for life; the hosanna must be
tried in the crucible of doubt, and so on in the same style.
But I don't meddle in that, I didn't create it, I am not
answerable for it. . . . Yes, till the secret is revealed, there
are two sorts of truth for me—one, their truth, yonder,
which I know nothing about so far, and the other my own.
And there is no knowing which will turn out the better.'

The devil (who is Ivan's reasoning *alter ego*) easily
disposes of God and enthrones the principle of 'all things
are lawful'. On the other hand, he adds at once even
more bitingly, alluding to Ivan's indirect participation in
Smerdyakov's crime: 'That is all very charming, but if
you want to swindle, why do you want a moral sanction
for doing it? But that's our modern Russian all over.
He can't bring himself to swindle without a moral
sanction. He is so in love with truth.'

Ivan's scepticism is not the result of a lukewarm
indifference, but of his intellectual integrity which is as
passionate in him as is his secret desire to go beyond the

intellect and to find something to believe in. That is why the devil taunts him:

'From the vehemence with which you deny my existence I am convinced that you believe in me.'

'Not in the slightest. I haven't a hundredth part of a grain of faith in you.'

'But you have the thousandth of a grain. Homoeopathic doses perhaps are the strongest. . . .'

'Not for one minute,' cried Ivan furiously. 'But I should like to believe in you,' he murmured strangely.

'I shall sow in you only a tiny grain of faith and it will grow into an oak-tree, and such an oak-tree that, sitting on it, you will long to enter the ranks of hermits and saintly women, for that is what you are secretly longing for. You'll dine on locusts, you'll wander into the wilderness to save your soul.'

Thus Ivan's secret leaks out. However honest his intellect may be, his spiritual longing with its own 'truth' is equally strong and honest. The result is self-division not only in his conscious, but also in his unconscious personality. So much so that whatever he does seems to be done only by one part of his ego.

IV

This is particularly noticeable in the murder of his father. The old Karamazov—like Raskolnikov's pawn-broker woman—was a human 'louse' whose existence did no good to any one, but plenty of harm to many. Ivan had suspected that the lackey Smerdyakov intended to murder the old sensualist in order to rob him, and he half-consciously approved of it. Without being fully aware of the fact, he infected Smerdyakov's mind with the principle of 'beyond good and evil', and thus gave him a logical sanction to commit the planned crime. He hated the flunkey, but something that was buried in the hidden layers of his self drew him towards him. When, shortly before the crime, he happened to pass by the bench on which the flunkey was sitting, he looked with repulsion at Smerdyakov's 'emasculate, sickly face, with the little curls combed forward on his forehead. His left eye winked and grinned as though to say, 'Where are you going? You won't pass by; you see that we two clever people have something to say to each other.' . . .

'Ivan shook. "Get away, you miserable idiot. What have I to do with you?" was on the tip of his tongue, but to his profound astonishment he heard himself say:

' "Is my father asleep or has he waked?"

'He asked the question softly and meekly, to his own surprise, and at once, again to his own surprise, sat down on the bench. For an instant he felt almost frightened; he remembered it afterwards. Smerdyakov stood facing him, looking at him with assurance and almost severity.'

The next morning Ivan, as though against his own will, left his father's house. The crime actually took place at night, while the old Karamazov, in one of his most libidinous moods, was expecting Grushenka. The infatuated Mitya happened to be round the house at the time of the murder. So the guilt fell upon him, not upon Smerdyakov. The reaction to the crime on the part of Ivan, who only *suspected* that Smerdyakov might be the murderer, was, however, analogous to Raskolnikov's state after the crime. We learn that he returned intensely nervous and dispirited. He believed, or forced himself to believe, that Mitya committed the murder after all. Yet he soon grew even more restless and anxious to find out the truth. 'Is it because I am as much a murderer at heart?' he asked himself. He visited Smerdyakov three times, partly in the hope of being reassured by him, and partly as though trying to bring into full consciousness those hidden wishes and impulses of his which had encouraged Smerdyakov to commit the crime. His three meetings with the sick murderer represent an extraordinary specimen of the double dialogue: one spoken, and the other remaining entirely 'between the lines'.

Something strange happened also to Smerdyakov. The crime perpetrated by him altered the very texture of his being. He fell ill. At the same time he seemed to have plunged into a new psychic realm in which human contacts as he had known them before mattered no longer. For the first time he now faced Ivan with arrogance, even with a kind of superiority, flinging at him words such as these:

'Here we are face to face; what's the use of going on keeping up a farce to each other? Are you still trying to throw it all on me, to my face? *You* murdered him; you are the real murderer. I was only your instrument, your faithful servant, and it was following your words I did it.'

' "Did it? Why did you murder him?" Ivan turned cold. Something seemed to give way in his brain, and he shuddered all over. Smerdyakov himself looked at him wonderingly; probably the genuineness of Ivan's horror struck him.

' "You were bold enough then. You said, 'everything is lawful', and how frightened you are now," Smerdyakov muttered in surprise.'

But he, too, reacted by unexpectedly handing over to Ivan the money he had stolen from the old Karamazov: 'I don't want it . . . I did have an idea of beginning a new life with that money in Moscow or, better still, abroad. I did dream of it, chiefly because "all things are lawful". That was quite right what you taught me, for you talked a lot to me about that. For if there's no everlasting God, there's no such thing as virtue, and there's no need of it. You were right there. So that's how I looked at it.'

'Did you come to that yourself?'

'With your guidance.'

'And now, I suppose, you believe in God, since you are giving back the money?'

'No, I don't believe,' whispered Smerdyakov.

'Then why are you giving it back?'

'Leave off . . . that's enough!' Smerdyakov waved his

hand again. 'You used to say yourself that everything was lawful, so now why are you so upset, too? You even want to give evidence against yourself . . .'

V

Like Raskolnikov and Stavrogin of the 'Confession', Ivan had decided to give evidence against himself. Juridically he was not guilty at all, but morally he considered himself guilty of his father's murder, although his logic repudiated any morality in the old sense. Smerdyakov hanged himself after the third and last interview with Ivan. Ivan, however, was plunged on the eve of Mitya's trial into a delirium in which his nightmare devil played the part of Mephistopheles—a *Russian* Mephistopheles.

The dialogue between Ivan and his devil is a unique chapter in literature. Its nervous agitated prose blends philosophic depth with a rare psychological intuition. We see in it human consciousness hurled to its farthest limits. And while the querying Ivan is engaged in his last fight to solve the problem of Value, the devil keeps on laughing and teasing—particularly when hinting at Ivan's decision to give evidence against himself at the trial.

'You are going to perform an act of heroic virtue, and you don't believe in virtue, that is what tortures you and makes you angry, that is why you are so vindictive. . . . No matter if they disbelieve you, you are going for the sake of principle. . . . Why do you want to go meddling, if your sacrifice is of no use to any one? Because you don't know yourself why you go! Oh, you'd give a great deal to know yourself why you go! . . . You must guess that for yourself. That's the riddle for you.'—This is how Ivan explains the gist of the dialogue to Alyosha.

The situation becomes even more paradoxical if one takes into account that Ivan hates his half-brother Mitya for whose sake he intends to accuse himself.

'I hate the monster,' he shouts to Alyosha. 'Let him rot

in Siberia.' Yet he adds: 'Oh, to-morrow I'll go, stand before them (the judge and the jury) and spit in their faces.'

'He will either rise up in the light of truth,' thought Alyosha, 'or he will perish in hate, revenging on himself and on every one his having served the cause he does not believe in.'

Ivan did give evidence against himself, 'spitting in their faces'. But in his rage and scorn he was far from rising in the light of truth. His reason had exhausted the depths of philosophic speculation, yet it did not bring him any nearer to the solution of the 'secret', of the two kinds of truth. It only brought him nearer to madness.

XI

CHRIST AND HIS DOUBLE

The Grand Inquisitor

I

IN Ivan Karamazov personal ideas and problems are turned into an intense spiritual drama. In his legend, *The Grand Inquisitor*, however, these cease to be personal and are projected upon humanity as a whole. The fate of mankind weighted down by the problem of Value and of a free choice between good and evil—such is the theme of this legend which contains some of the finest pages Dostoevsky ever wrote. It was in his *Notes from the Underworld* that he stressed the freedom of volition at all cost. Yet even in his confused story, *The Landlady*, written before he was sent to Siberia, he showed—psychologically—that such freedom can often become a burden, incompatible with human nature. He deepened this motive in his novels and brought it to a climax in Ivan's Legend.

To Ivan, as to Dostoevsky, Christ was the most perfect embodiment of inner freedom. Being Himself free, He wanted all men to be free, to follow Him and His way of life of their own will: without any compulsion or intimidation, without bribes (such as the promise of heaven) and even without any guarantee that the Value revealed by Him was 'within the Truth'. Such an ideal proved, however, beyond men's power. They may be rebellious by nature, but once they have won what they regard as freedom, their first care is to get rid of it. For its burden is heavier than slavery.

This applies particularly to man's inner freedom of choice between good and evil. So much so that the Christian Church has considered it necessary to limit and supervise human conscience itself. That was why Dostoevsky (whose attitude towards Catholicism was rather prejudiced) turned Ivan's Grand Inquisitor into a symbol of Roman Catholic theocracy, based on authority, on spiritual and moral coercion. But the essence of true religion should always be inner freedom. Any denial of such freedom was regarded by Dostoevsky as pseudo-religion, as atheism in disguise. The Grand Inquisitor himself is the greatest opponent of freedom, but for his own reasons. In order to make these clear, Ivan confronts him with Christ Himself whom the Inquisitor still acknowledges in name, but denies in spirit. Instead of being His representative, he is only His opposite, His 'double'.

The originality and depth of the legend consists in the fact that both Christ and His 'double' meet as equals, anxious to help and to save humanity. The Grand Inquisitor knows mankind too well to expect anything from it. He takes men for what they are worth and treats them as they deserve. He despises them. At the same time he is full of solicitude for the millions of cowards and sinners entrusted to his care. It is out of pity that he wants to ease their lot on earth. And he hopes to achieve this by *lowering* their consciousness to that level on which he could deprive them of inner freedom, of all moral responsibility, and thus impose upon them the 'happiness of babes'.

His edifice, based on authority, miracle, and mystery, is already far advanced when Christ's sudden reappearance endangers the entire structure. Christ had committed once before an unpardonable mistake. He had rated men too highly and expected the impossible from them: the strength to endure His own freedom. But His gospel failed to make humanity either free or happy. This is why the Grand Inquisitor wants to correct His work. He wants to see men at least happy—happy at the expense of freedom.

Such is the dilemma when Christ and His double meet face to face.

II

Ivan Karamazov begins his legend with the assumption that Christ returned to earth and appeared in Seville at the time of the Holy Inquisition. He came 'softly, unobserved, and yet, strange to say, every one recognized Him'. Moving through the crowd, blessing and healing, He raises a girl from the dead at the very moment when the Grand Inquisitor—'an old man, almost ninety, tall and erect, with a withered face and sunken eyes, in which there is still a gleam of light'—is passing by. The Inquisitor witnesses the miracle. And while the amazed crowd is weeping at Christ's feet, he coldly orders his guards to throw Him into the dungeon. The Inquisitor knows whom he has arrested. He also knows why he has done it. He himself does not believe either in God or in Christ. Regarding the existence of men as something meaningless, as a plaything of circumstances, illusions, and delusions, he freezes in his inner vacuum, but is strong enough to face and to endure it. And while keeping this knowledge to himself, he is all the more anxious to impose upon mankind a comfortable lie, in order to protect them from his own unhappiness.

The stern Inquisitor is thus rightly perturbed by the return of Christ. But before burning Him at the stake *ad majorem Dei gloriam*, he visits his Prisoner at night: not so much to tell Christ of the fate awaiting Him in the morning, as in order to challenge Him and justify before Him his own action. Under the vaults of the prison, the nonagenarian looks into His gentle eyes, and begins piling reproach on reproach.

'Is it Thou? Thou? Do not answer, be silent. What canst Thou say, indeed? And Thou hast no right to add anything to what Thou hast said of old. Why, then, art Thou come to hinder us? Hast Thou the right to reveal to us one of the mysteries of that world from which Thou hast come? No, Thou hast not; that Thou mayest not add to what has been said of old, and mayest not take from men the freedom which Thou didst exalt when Thou wast on earth. Whatsoever Thou revealest anew will encroach on men's freedom of faith; for it will be manifest as a miracle, and the freedom of their faith was dearer to Thee than anything in those days fifteen hundred years ago. Didst Thou not often say then, "I will make you free"? But now Thou hast seen these "free" men. . . . Yes, we have paid dearly for it. For fifteen centuries we have been wrestling with Thy freedom.'

Instead of the ancient Law which dictated by force what was good and what was evil, Christ had transferred all the values and valuations into the heart of each individual, whose conscience alone now had to decide—to decide in complete freedom—whether to follow Him or not. But in doing this He had forgotten that 'man prefers peace, and even death, to freedom of choice in good and evil'. Besides, where is the guarantee that Christ and the Value bequeathed by Him to humanity are inside and not outside the Truth? Could man, weak and rebellious as he is, ever accept Him without doubts and perplexities, and, above all, without coercion? Could he ever rise to God through love and freedom as taught by Christ?

'Didst Thou not know that he would at last reject even Thy image and Thy truth, if he is weighed down with the fearful burden of free choice? They will not have been left in greater confusion and suffering than Thou hast caused, laying upon them so many cares and unanswerable problems . . .'

Respecting man less than He did, Christ would have asked less of him. And 'that would have been more like love, for his burden would have been lighter'. As it is, Christ's heroic path can only be entered upon by the few elect—by those only who are strong enough to accept and to endure His inner freedom. But if this be so, where

then is justice? Did Christ come for the sake of the
chosen few, leaving the rest to their own fate? And what
would happen to the countless millions of those weaklings
if the Grand Inquisitor did not take care of them, having
sacrificed everything, even truth, to the cause of their
peace and happiness? What would become of them, had
he not rejected Christ for the sake of official Christianity?

III

The Inquisitor is thus, like Ivan, unwilling to take his
place among the elect, if at the same time 'millions of
creatures have been created as a mockery'. He repudiates
Christ not for personal reasons, but out of pity for mankind. His injured sense of justice makes him throw in
his lot with the doomed millions rather than sing hosanna
in the company of the few elect.

'Thy great prophet tells in vision and image that he
saw all those who took part in the first resurrection, and
that there were of each tribe twelve thousand. They
had borne Thy cross, they had endured scores of years
in the barren, hungry wilderness, living upon locusts and
roots—and Thou mayest indeed point with pride at those
children of freedom, of free love, of free and splendid
sacrifice for Thy name. But remember that they were
only some thousands; and what of the rest? And how
are the other weak ones to blame, because they could
not endure what the strong have endured? How is the
weak soul to blame that it is unable to receive such
terrible gifts?'

'Canst Thou simply come to the elect and for the elect?
But if so, it is a mystery and we cannot understand it.
And if so, we too have a right to preach a mystery, and
to teach them that it is not free judgment of their hearts,
not love that matters, but a mystery which they must
follow blindly, even against their conscience.'

It was the care for the weak ones which made the
Grand Inquisitor substitute a fake for Christ. Knowing

that they would never be ripe for free choice and judgment, he invested himself with the authority of an 'infallible' spirit who alone guards the mystery of good and evil, and is therefore entitled to hold in pawn the conscience of men—for their own benefit. He is so sure of his power that he smiles even at those who rebel against him in the name of science and reason. Men want to be saved first of all from themselves, and that is what science and reason can never achieve. He alone hopes to achieve it—by correcting Christ's work in the sense of the three temptations in the desert, i.e. by enslaving men's conscience and relieving them of their freedom for ever.

'We have corrected Thy work and have founded it upon *miracle*, *mystery*, and *authority*. And men rejoiced that they were again led like sheep, and that the terrible gift that had brought them such suffering was, at last, lifted from their hearts. Were we right teaching them this? . . . Did we not love mankind, so meekly acknowledging their feebleness, lovingly lightening their burden, and permitting their weak nature even sin with our sanction?'

IV

While disclosing the secret that he himself is on the side of Antichrist (who is the negation of spiritual freedom), the Grand Inquisitor draws before his silently listening Prisoner some perspectives and visions of the future. Men will still continue to rebel for a while. But the burden of freedom on the one hand, and science and mere reason on the other, will bring about so many insoluble riddles, such inner and external chaos, that the strongest ones will destroy themselves, whereas the weak ones will begin destroying each other. Eventually they will crawl to the Inquisitor's feet and whine: 'Yes, you were right, you alone possess His mystery, and we come back to you, save us from ourselves.' And then the 'infallible' Grand Inquisitor of the future will become master of the world, which he will organize on the lines of obedience and depersonalization. Once deprived of inner freedom, mankind will be *compelled* to become happy —by conforming to ruthless external dictates of what is good and what is evil *for all*.[1] Theirs will be the happiness of infants who have no worries, no inner responsibilities. If any disturbing questions should ever crop up with some of them, the Inquisitor will know what to answer and what to do in order to restore their happiness. And so all will be 'happy'—all except those few who will rule over them and guard the secret.

'There will be thousands of millions of happy babes, and a hundred thousand of sufferers who have taken upon themselves the curse of the knowledge of good and evil. Peacefully they will die, peacefully they will expire in Thy name, and beyond the grave they will find nothing but death. But we shall keep the secret, and for their happiness we shall allure them with the reward of heaven and eternity. For if there were anything in the other world, it certainly would not be for such as they. . . .'

To love the perfect man, the new Adam, as Christ preached him is easy. What is difficult is to love the man as he is—to love those whom one cannot respect. The Grand Inquisitor pities humanity precisely because it is so miserable, so abject in its weakness, in its moral squalor and meanness. His 'love' is utterly different from Christ's love of mankind, yet in its own way it is heroic. That is why he talks to Christ as an equal and challenges Him as an equal.

'It is prophesied that Thou wilt come again in victory, Thou wilt come with Thy chosen, the proud and strong; they will say that they have only saved themselves, but we have saved all. Then I will stand up and point out

[1] His edifice of future happiness is analogous to the one proposed by the nihilist Shigalyov and dreamed of by Verkhovensky in *The Possessed*. Faked socialism and faked Christianity thus meet and coincide.

to Thee the thousand millions of happy children who
have known no sin. And we, who have taken their sins
upon us for their happiness, will stand up before Thee
and say: "Judge us if Thou canst and darest." Know
that I fear Thee not. Know that I too have been in the
wilderness. I too have lived on roots and locusts, I too
prized the freedom with which Thou hast blessed men,
and I too was striving to stand among the elect, among
the strong and powerful, thirsting to "make up the
number". But I awakened and would not serve madness.
I turned back and joined the ranks of those *who have
corrected Thy work*. I left the proud and went back to
the humble, for the happiness of the humble.'

V

Words such as these can only be born of incredible
despair, spite, and pity. The man uttering them is a
saint and a martyr without faith, and this makes his
tragedy even greater. Yet he turns suffering itself into a
privilege to which are entitled only those supermen who
are strong enough not to be crushed by their own knowledge and burden. They will pay full price for it. But
they will also rule the world, jealously guarding their own
secret on the one hand, and the happiness of the masses
on the other. The masses—all the countless 'many-too-
many'—have no right to suffer. They must be spared
the ordeal. Any one who endangers their organized
happiness deserves to be punished as an enemy of mankind, whatever his intentions. And the greatest danger
is Christ with His terrible gift of inner freedom. That
is why the Grand Inquisitor is determined to burn Him,
in order to save humanity from His influence once and
for all.

'What I say to Thee will come to pass, and our dominion
will be built up. I repeat, to-morrow Thou shalt see that
obedient flock who, at a sign from me, will hasten to
heap the hot cinders about the pile on which I shall burn

Thee for coming to hinder us. For if any one has ever
deserved our fires it is Thou. To-morrow I shall burn
Thee. *Dixi*.'

He stops and waits for an answer from his Prisoner,
who all the while has been silently looking into his face.
Without uttering a word, Christ goes up to him and kisses
him on his pale and bloodless lips.

The Inquisitor shudders. Then he opens the prison
door:

'Go, and come no more . . . come not at all, never,
never!'

Christ silently goes out and vanishes into the dark
alleys of the town.

It is not only this paradoxical end, but the entire
Legend that makes one wonder: On whose side is the
truth? Is it on the side of Christ or of His double? The
whole of *The Grand Inquisitor* is the soliloquy of a man
whose divided consciousness is unable to side either with
Christ or with His opposite. And the man was Dostoevsky
himself. Having found no answer in Ivan, he looked for
it in another direction and thus created the figure of
Father Zosima.

XII

TOWARDS A SYNTHESIS

IN Ivan Karamazov a double conflict takes place. The hatred he bears his father and his half-brother Mitya (both of whom he unconsciously helps to ruin) is of a nature that modern psycho-analysis would easily account for. But parallel with this, his spiritual travail reaches a tension verging on madness. In this respect Ivan's 'Grand Inquisitor' and his nightmare talk with the devil complete each other. Both embody his 'rebellion' and bring to a head the two aspects of Dostoevsky's main theme: the problem of Value on the one hand, and that of inner Freedom on the other.

Having started with man's self-will and pursued it to the end, Dostoevsky found on that path nothing but destruction, self-destruction, and moral anarchy in which each man becomes a law unto himself. He regarded the ultimate relativity of values as untenable on the plane of spirit, although on the social plane (which is a compromise between one's personal and the collective utility) it might be quite successful, if kept within certain boundaries. A wise legislation could eradicate a number of major evils from our social life, without even touching upon the metaphysical problem of evil itself. Nor does yet absence of pain and suffering in the social sphere imply their absence in the sphere of the spirit where each individual has to cope at his own risk with such eternal dilemmas as God, Value, Freedom, and Immortality.

According to Dostoevsky, these are but four aspects of one and the same dilemma and struggle: the struggle for an ultimate meaning of life. Having reached that stage of consciousness where life can be accepted only on condition that there *is* such a meaning in it, man postulates not only God and a supreme Value, but also that inner independence without which a free choice between good and evil would be impossible. This may serve, perhaps, as a sufficient metaphysical apology for the existence of evil. If there was only good in this world, there would be no choice and hence no freedom, for men would be unavoidably good.

Here we arrive, however, at another interesting conflict. While our spirit accepts evil for the sake of man's inner freedom, our moral sense may at the same time violently protest and rebel against the existence of evil. The depth of Ivan's psychology lies precisely in this clash between the spiritual and the purely moral planes. He demands Christ's ideal of inner freedom, and yet rebels against evil, without which such freedom would be impossible. He admits the existence of God, but rejects the iniquitous and suffering world created by God: he hands in his 'entrance ticket'.

Ivan's struggle came to no conclusion. But Ivan was Dostoevsky himself, or at least one of his 'doubles'. And Dostoevsky had to find an answer which would prevent him from handing in his own 'entrance ticket'. In doing so, he embarked upon further uncertainties, and was aware of it. But for this very reason he insisted all the more passionately on the need for that ultimate meaning of life which is inseparable from one's belief in God, Freedom, and Immortality. Thus in his *Journal of an Author* he argued that 'without a superior idea cannot exist either the Individual or the Nation. But here, on earth, we have only one superior idea—and this is the idea of the *immortality of the soul*, because all superior ideas have their source in this idea'. And again (quite in contrast to Versilov's dream): 'The idea that the life of mankind is only a flash and that all will be reduced to nothing, kills even one's love for mankind. The consciousness that one cannot give any help to suffering humanity can change the love that you had for mankind into hatred of mankind. I even assert that love of mankind is in general but little comprehensible and beyond the grasp of the human soul. This love can only be justified by the feeling which is derived from the belief in the immortality of the soul. Without the conviction that our soul is immortal, the attachment of man to this planet would vanish, and the loss of a higher meaning of life would lead undoubtedly to suicide.'

The promise of personal immortality has been used hitherto as a solace and compensation for the miseries of this life. Dostoevsky reversed the situation. No matter whether he entirely believed or not in God and immortality, he postulated both as a condition for the fullness of our earthly existence itself. God and immortality must exist, for otherwise a man with a highly developed consciousness could not and indeed *ought not* to accept his own existence. He wrote at length about this in his novels, his *Journal*, and in his private correspondence. What interests us here, however, is mainly his attempts to express these ideas in terms of art, that is, in the characters of his novels.

II

Like many other Russian authors, Dostoevsky is convincing whenever he depicts negative characters. His portraits of their opposites are, however, less numerous and, on the whole, less successful. Prince Myshkin is with all his charm an anaemic figure, unable to will and to act. There is something remote and piously stylized about Makar Ivanovitch in *A Raw Youth*. Father Zosima and his disciple, Alyosha, may not be quite convincing either, but they are at least more robust, more 'normal'. And both are assigned a vital part in *The Brothers Karamazov*.

Father Zosima is an active counterpart of Myshkin. He is not an abstraction, nor a mere mouthpiece of the

author, although he embodies the religious ideal of
Dostoevsky himself. André Gide's dictum that Dostoevsky 'leads us if not to anarchy, to a sort of Buddhism,
or at least quietism', can perhaps be applied to Myshkin,
but not to Zosima. Zosima's path is action in accordance
with that spiritual self-realization which is beyond
Raskolnikov's self-will or the rebellion of Ivan Karamazov. Or is it *before* it? The reader is not sufficiently
enlightened upon this matter. The interpolated confession and teaching of Zosima are not so much an overcoming as an antithesis of Ivan's 'Pro and Contra'. And
they are much less vigorous, less complete. Nor do we
know anything about the previous phases of Zosima's
inner life. Did he have to pass through the same chaos
of 'doubles' as Stavrogin and Ivan? And if so, how did
he conquer it? In short, is his serene simplicity one that
comes before or after complexity? His conversion, as
presented in the novel, cannot be considered a sufficient
answer. Besides, it is shown not as a process, but—
retrospectively—as a suddenly accomplished fact.

No wonder that Zosima is also more didactic than
any character in Dostoevsky's novels. On the other
hand, the ideal he stands for is perhaps too big to be
embodied in concrete terms: as flesh and blood. This
may be the reason why the author preferred to interpolate
it in the form of theory and exhortation—largely in the
manner of a famous eighteenth-century monk, Tikhon
Zadonsky. What makes matters even somewhat confused
is Zosima's formula of the Church Universal, which is
too theological to be art, and too pregnant with vital
thought to coincide with any official theology. In addition, there were also outward influences and stimuli.
The young philosopher Vladimir Solovyov was one of
them. Fresh from Moscow, he gave in the winter of
1877-8 a course of lectures on the destinies of mankind. Dostoevsky was among his listeners and he
probably moulded, to some extent, at least a few of

his own ideas about the Church Universal on those of Solovyov.

As a great artist, he was anxious to show the working of such ideas through living characters. He found a suitable model for his *starets* (Elder) Zosima in Father Ambrosius—a monk of the Optina Monastery, which he and Solovyov visited in June 1878. In spite of that, Zosima's personality and teaching can be summed up as Dostoevsky's own vision of the new integrated man to come. It is an answer to Ivan's negation and also an attempt at a Christian synthesis of life—a synthesis not in the name of any official Christianity, but rather in the name of Christ as he understood Him. And his final approach to Christ has nothing to do with any ascetic aversion to life and earth. Just the reverse. Asceticism usually excludes the fullness of life. It often excludes also the beauty of life. Preoccupied chiefly with one's personal salvation, it is in danger of degenerating into mean egotism, or into the complacently arrogant 'Are you saved?' business. What Dostoevsky wanted was not asceticism (whether Christian or otherwise), but the highest intensity of life. His own Christian ideal can be defined above all as affirmation and personal expansion through universal sympathy. Instead of excluding and condemning various aspects of life, it includes and transmutes them. The essence of his Christianity is not gloom or sadness, but joy and beauty. This is why Father Zosima's message is as serene as his entire personality.

It should be stressed again that this message is only partly embodied in the novel. But even so it gives one a fairly reliable idea of the author's own trend after his spiritual 'storm and stress' period, although it should not be entirely identified with his convictions. It rather shows the convictions he *wanted* to have. Still, it is most important for an understanding of the final phase of Dostoevsky the man and the novelist. Having started his career with 'rebellion', he ended it with affirmation (as distinct from resignation). And in his opinion affirmation was inseparable from sympathy and love. 'Love all God's creation and every grain of sand in it,' he says through his mouthpiece Zosima. 'Love every leaf, every ray of God's light. If you love everything, you will perceive the divine mystery of things.' And on another occasion: 'God took seeds from different worlds and sowed them on this earth, and his garden grew up and everything came up that could come up, but what grows, lives and is alive only through the feeling of its contact with other mysterious worlds. If that feeling grows weak or is destroyed in you, the heavenly growth will die in you. Then you will be indifferent to life and even grow to hate it.'

III

As if aware of the much too didactic propensity of Zosima, Dostoevsky gave us in Alyosha Karamazov the same type of consciousness, but still in the making. Alyosha was not entirely a product of Dostoevsky's imagination. He is supposed to have modelled him on a friend he had known in his youth. On the other hand, Mgr. d'Herbigny assures us in his book, *Un Newman russe*, that the actual prototype of Alyosha was Vladimir Solovyov. Be this as it may, Alyosha is another antipodes of Ivan.

It is idle to speculate about the part he would have played in the projected *Life of a Great Sinner*, had Dostoevsky had time to write it. As it is, Alyosha impresses us as being all of a piece. His inner balance or harmony has not yet passed through doubts and sin—so familiar to Dostoevsky. But there are indications that these were latent in him: he could not help being a Karamazov, after all. Yet instead of falling a prey to them, he instinctively sublimates them. He is not for nothing a disciple of Zosima. And Zosima's guidance finds a counterpart, as it were, in Alyosha's friendship with a crowd of wonderfully described schoolboys. The section dealing with them is one of the most refreshing in the book. Alyosha passes through a sudden crisis after Zosima's death. But in the beautiful chapter, 'Cana of Galilee', his irrational contact with 'other mysterious worlds' restores him to life, to this earth, and to himself.

'He went quickly down; his soul overflowing with rapture, yearned for freedom, space, openness. The vault of heaven, full of soft, shining stars, stretched vast and fathomless above him. The Milky Way ran in two pale streams from the zenith to horizon. The fresh, motionless, still night enfolded the earth. The white towers and golden domes of the cathedral gleamed out against the sapphire sky. The gorgeous autumn flowers in the beds around the house were slumbering till morning. The silence of earth seemed to melt into the silence of the heavens. The mystery of earth was one with the mystery of the stars. Alyosha stood, gazed, and suddenly threw himself down on the earth. He did not know why he embraced it. He could not have told why he longed so irresistibly to kiss it, to kiss it all. But he kissed it weeping, sobbing and watering it with his tears, and vowed passionately to love it, to love it for ever. . . . In his rapture he was weeping even over those stars which were shining to him from the abyss of space and he was not ashamed of that ecstasy. There seemed to be threads from all those innumerable worlds of God, linking his soul to them, and it was trembling all over in 'contact with other worlds'. He longed to forgive every one and everything. With every instance he felt clearly and, as it were, tangibly, that something firm and unshakable as that vault of heaven had entered into his soul. It was as though some idea had seized the sovereignty of his mind —and it was for all his life and for ever and ever.'

IV

The final note of Dostoevsky's work and struggle is a new fullness of existence which man should reach by conquering and re-creating himself. Unable to accept life as something accidental and meaningless, he was bound to visualize it only in the light of its highest significance. If man is not a casual product of casual blind forces, then his individual consciousness is necessarily part and parcel of the creative consciousness behind the Universe. His inner struggle is then a part of the great world-drama; and his ascent, his victories and defeats, may have consequences which go far beyond his personal destiny—no matter whether he knows it or not. We are here to be helpers of God. And each of us is responsible, in his own way, for the whole of life, responsible for all and everything.

Dostoevsky knew only too well that our life becomes sterile and shallow if it is cut off from its deeper transcendental roots. So his quest for God was in essence a quest for the highest fulfilment of man on earth—a fulfilment through an integration of life, religion, and beauty. He even insisted that 'beauty will save the world'. Knowing that morality itself, if devoid of beauty, becomes a distortion—and often a fatal distortion—of life, he eventually refused to separate the 'good' from the 'beautiful'. He saw them reunited on that religious plane towards which he strove.

It was mainly such a vision of life that made him turn with vehemence against the new acquisitive bourgeoisie on the one hand, and the complacent positivist radicals on the other. Whether rightly or wrongly, he regarded both as equally superficial, meanly utilitarian, and therefore dangerous to the aspirations of man's spirit. It goes without saying that his hatred of Belinsky had something to do with it. And is it possible to depict a more despicable (and unfair) figure of a budding Russian radical than

Rakitin in *The Brothers Karamazov*? Its only justification is that Rakitin's intellectual smugness was also meant to be the opposite of the profound inner quest of Ivan, of Mitya's 'vexation of the spirit' (while in prison), and of Alyosha's intuitive wisdom.

What Dostoevsky refused to accept, was an easily gained truth and experience. As a great enemy of intellectual, emotional and spiritual sloth, he always preferred to face the most dangerous consequences rather than stop half-way. And his ridiculing of all sorts of 'Claude Bernards' in *The Brothers Karamazov* is not jeering at science, but at the camp-followers of popularized would-be-science with its ready-made slogans and formulae. Having striven all his life in order to unravel the riddle of man, he knew the price required by such a task. How big the price was, can be gathered from the phases of his own spiritual travail and struggle—phases which are so powerfully recorded in his literary work.

XIII

THE 'RUSSIAN IDEA', REVOLUTION
AND RELIGION

I

DOSTOEVSKY'S preoccupation with the 'inner man' did not detract his interest from those more external problems of life which he considered vital. He referred to them, not only in his novels, but often discussed them at length in his causeries and articles. Quite a number of these appeared in *Vremia* and *Epokha*, in Prince Meshchersky's *Grazhdanin* ('The Citizen'), and particularly in his personal *Journal of an Author*, where he dealt with all sorts of 'accursed problems', then current in Russia. Politics, literature, the peasantry, the intelligentsia, the Russo-Turkish War, the Slavs, exceptional law cases, social and psychological anomalies—they all came in for much provocative criticism. Yet, what strikes one in that miscellany, apart from Dostoevsky's broadness of interests, are his frequent contradictions. Thus, in spite of his universal sympathies, he did not mind flirting with the Tsarist imperialism in the Near East. The prospect of Constantinople as a Russian city even became one of his pet obsessions which he tried to justify by numerous arguments. His attitude towards the Poles and the Jews was often biased, to say the least. Nor was he averse to hobnobbing with the official Church authorities whose tolerance in those days was far from exemplary. But whatever his ideological and emotional vagaries, he remained consistent at least with regard to his central themes: the 'Russian Idea', the problem of revolution, of socialism (as he understood it), of culture and religion.

The earliest roots of the Russian Idea, formulated by the Slavophils and modified by Dostoevsky, go as far back as Moscovite Russia which, after the fall of Constantinople, regarded herself as the 'Third Rome', radiating the only true Christian faith for the benefit and salvation of the world. In the nineteenth century this self-righteous attitude assumed a frankly messianic aspect, not only on the religious, but—strange to say—even on the irreligious plane. The innate Russian universalism, so different from the aggressive exclusiveness of the Germans, found in the cultural and social thought of nineteenth-century Russia two antagonistic directions. The conservative Slavophils hoped (quite in the old Moscow tradition) to save Europe from materialism by revealing to her the Russo-Christian trend of civilization. The revolutionary Westerners, however, dreamed of a universal socialist millennium which might be started by the Russian masses—also for the benefit of the world.

Devoid of the training in economic and social principles as understood to-day, Dostoevsky was the more inclined to rely on his intuitions, even on his wishful thinking. The idea of man being a mere product of economic factors, for example, would have seemed to him an insult and even something illogical, since it was man who produced and shaped those factors, for which reason he must come prior to them. Nor did he believe in the efficacy of a purely external reshuffling of wealth. He wanted not only a quantitative, but a qualitative change. What he thought of a mere quantitative revolution, whether achieved through violence or otherwise, he said plainly enough in *The Possessed* and in *The Grand Inquisitor*. 'Human nature is not taken into account . . . they (the pseudo-revolutionaries) do not want a living soul. And so it comes in the end to their reducing everything to the building of walls and passages in a phalanstery. Logic presupposes three possibilities, but there are millions! Cut away a million and reduce it all to a question of comfort! That is the easiest solution of the problem. . . . The whole secret of life on two pages of print!' (*The Possessed*). Aiming at the integrated and not the standardized man, Dostoevsky saw the only possibility of a *creative* change on the spiritual plane. Hence his interest in religion. Hence his aversion to all those doctrines, systems and ideas in which there was no room for one's freedom of conscience, or for what he regarded as the irrational in a supranormal sense.

II

Dostoevsky's irrational trend was fostered not only by his innate inclinations, but even by his intellect which was sharp enough to see its own limitations. Far from rejecting the rational element in man, he only relegated it to its proper sphere. Since mere logic and reason had proved unable to cope with the ultimate problems of man's existence, he either had to give up his quest, or else to explore some other means of cognition. He adopted the second course, even if this involved the element of faith—that is, the will to accept certain attitudes and probabilities without or perhaps against the sanction of his 'Euclidean' intellect. Yet the latter kept on rebelling in the name of its own honesty, as distinct from Dostoevsky's spiritual honesty which usually went in the opposite direction, thus making his cleavage all the greater.

The question which arises is whether Dostoevsky had ever gone beyond his passionate will to believe. A careful study of his novels and correspondence only confirms the difficulty he had in fighting his own 'crucible of doubts', his latent nihilism. Even the Russian Idea, as formulated by him in the end, was above all a projection of his desire to integrate some of those contrasts and conflicts within himself which threatened to undermine his personality. Identifying his own needs and wishes with the prospective mission of his country, he could not help but see her as a universal peace-maker, reconciling all the contrasts—Russian and European—in a higher synthesis to come.

Such an attitude demanded, however, that tolerant view of the European West which he finally adopted. In spite of his loathing of Western philistinism, he could hardly dismiss the cultural achievements of the European past. In fact, he admired them, even if they seemed to him more like a 'beautiful cemetery'—a view expressed clearly enough through Versilov and Ivan Karamazov. But if so, the mission of Russia as he saw or wished to see it, assumed an all the greater significance. Her destiny was, in short, to reveal to Europe a new scale of values, and the ideal of a true integrated unity of mankind, as distinct from a compulsory external unification. Outside and apart from such a unity Dostoevsky saw no creative future either for Russia or mankind as a whole, but only a rapidly growing Tower of Babel, whose very productivity was doomed to hasten its ruin.

It was for this reason that he wrote: 'The future Russian Idea is not yet born, but the entire earth awaits it in pain and suffering.' And again (in his *Journal of an Author*): 'I make no attempt to compare Russia with the Western nations in the matter of economic and scientific renown. I only say that the Russian people are perhaps among all nations the most capable of upholding the ideal of universal union of mankind, of brotherly love, of the calm conception which forgives contrasts. This is not an economic, but a moral trait.' In his Pushkin speech he went even further, when saying that 'to a true Russian Europe and the destiny of all the mighty Aryan [*sic*] family are as dear as Russia herself; because our destiny is universality won not by the sword, but by the strength of brotherhood and our fraternal aspirations, to reunite mankind. And, in course of time, I believe that we shall, without exception, understand that to be a Russian does indeed mean to aspire finally to reconcile the contradictions of Europe, to show the end of our European yearning in our Russian soul, omni-human and all-uniting, to include within our soul by brotherly love all our brethren, and at last it may be, to pronounce the final word of the great general harmony, of the general brotherly communion of all nations in accordance with the law and the gospel of Christ.'

III

Passages such as this may seem—especially in the light of our present-day history—mere rhetoric. Yet to a Russian they still can mean something that might some time become real. Dostoevsky himself was so much carried away by longings of this kind as to over-simplify the complicated problems of revolution on the one hand, and of human unity on the other. No one has given us a deeper insight into the inner workings of a metaphysical rebel than Dostoevsky. But if a concrete social revolution is treated first of all from a metaphysical and not from a social-economic angle, we are likely to confuse the issues. Theoretically one is quite entitled to abhor the revolution on account of its violence. Yet even from a moral standpoint the injustice and cruelty caused by a revolution may be smaller, much smaller, than the perpetuation of that injustice against which one rebels. And we all know how strong the tendency towards such a perpetuation—in the social and economic sphere—can be.

We are now familiar with the deeper psychological and spiritual reasons which made Dostoevsky condemn the revolutionaries of the Nechayev type and to proclaim them apostles of half-truths: that 'most terrible scourge of humanity, unknown up to this century, and worse than plague, famine, or war' (*The Possessed*). But is it not another half-truth to reduce all the revolutionaries, even those burning with the most unselfish thirst for justice, to such a common denominator? Dostoevsky's assertion that the 'socialism of the Russian people is expressed neither in communistic doctrines, nor by any mechanical formulae, but by its deep longing for a universal union in the name of Christ', may sound all right in theory. But what is one to do if in practice such a union lags behind, while the social-economic contrasts and iniquities are growing to breaking-point? Once such a point has been reached, an explosion is inevitable, metaphysics or no.

This does not mean that on his own plane Dostoevsky was wrong when stressing the need of and the hope for an inner union. The question which arises is whether such inner unity can be achieved without a previous or at least a parallel change in those conditions which hamper any unity at all. Dostoevsky offered no practical answer. Still, the fact that he drew a line between the religious and irreligious types of socialism, undoubtedly points to two different trends, two different types of consciousness. This brings us, however, once more to the problem of society and religion on the one hand, and to the entire spiritual crisis of our times on the other.

IV

The essence of the present-day crisis can perhaps best be defined as humanism turning against itself. Humanism and the Renaissance were responsible for the emancipation of the European individual—a process which went hand in hand with the secularization of Western European thought and culture. The medieval man felt at peace, because he relied on the authority of the Church and the Bible. The man of our historical period was plunged, however, into all sorts of uncertainties as soon as he began to rely exclusively on his logic and reason. He fell back upon himself, stumbling over one insoluble problem after the other. Individualism let loose turned in the end into that wild competition and war of all against all which reached its climax in the more recent phases of our capitalist society. Instead of serving mankind, our tremendous capitalist system, severed from inner values, began to develop at the expense of mankind. Parallel with that, the accelerated pace of our mechanical civilization grew at the expense of creative culture. At last it turned, in a most destructive manner, against our entire cultural heritage. It turned, moreover, against humanity itself, now being destroyed by the perfection of its own science and technique, while the individual himself is threatened by a growing process of standardization. Humanism, which once had started with the affirmation of the individual, has now landed not only individuals but entire nations in mutual destruction and self-destruction, as though illustrating Raskolnikov's dream in Siberia.

Aware of the inner causes of the impending calamity, Dostoevsky, the psychologist, did his uttermost to diagnose it and to warn us. Apart from our mechanical Tower of Babel, it was also the collectivist tendency of our age which filled him, as it did so many other Europeans, with apprehension. Yet it was not collectivism itself he was afraid of, but the wrong, purely quantitative and utilitarian direction which it might take. Unable to visualize human society otherwise than in terms of an organism united from within, he distrusted all the more those trends and doctrines which experimented upon humanity as a mere organization, substituting compulsory uniformity for real unity.

This may provide an additional explanation for his call to religion. It was not a 'call back', but rather forward, to that religion without which no society could find enough inner coherence to endure. But religion and especially Christianity as he understood it was the reverse of that mental and moral sloth which so frequently passes for it nowadays. It also demanded depth, spiritual daring and that warm and active love without which even the most efficient society remains only a formal organization. It was here that Dostoevsky touched, however briefly, upon one of the cardinal problems of our age—the problem of Christianity and Socialism. He himself actually wished for a union between the two, as though realizing that outside of such a union Christianity is doomed to become an even greater sham than it is at present.

Curiously enough, even the violent revolution of 1917 would hardly have succeeded had it not also been motivated by that universalism which Dostoevsky regarded as the very quintessence of the Russian national character. We need not be unduly disturbed even by its anti-religious tendencies. Underneath its anti-religious surface, there was the profoundly Christian impulse of justice and the brotherhood of man at a time when 'Christian' Europe represented the greatest possible negation of Christianity in practice.

There certainly is something abnormal in the fact that such an essentially Christian current as Socialism is taking place outside or even against the Christian churches. We are perhaps not wrong if we say that present-day Russia rejected the reactionary official Christianity not because it was Christian, but because—in practice—it was not Christian enough, not Christian at all. She rejected it indeed for moral reasons. But the very passion with which she did this may indicate a roundabout way to a truer and more genuine Christianity in practice than mankind has known hitherto.

A *rapprochement* between Socialism and Christianity is not only desirable, but necessary. And if it does not take place at the right time and in the right direction, then such a delay may ultimately become fatal for both. We stand at present at the most ominous cross-roads in history. Dostoevsky's diagnosis can help us to see at least some of its aspects in the right perspective, and to shape out of our present chaos something better than what we are leaving behind.

CONCLUSION

DOSTOEVSKY is one of those authors the interest in whom may fluctuate but will hardly ever die out. A great writer and seeker in one, he deepened our awareness of man and life to such an extent that his work forms a landmark not only in the European novel, but also in the European consciousness. His psychological dissections may at times be disturbing. The same applies to his apocalyptic mentality. On the other hand, it is precisely because of these qualities that Dostoevsky is so revealing, and stimulating. Those who read him in a creative way will certainly derive more benefit from him than from any other modern. In addition, he can provide an introduction to some basic Russian features, as well as to those wider issues which make Russia so important a complement to the rest of Europe, perhaps of the world.

But let us quote what a contemporary European, Count H. Keyserling, says about this in his *Europe*: 'Even independently of its present function as a historic symbol, Russia has a great significance for Europe; that influence which it exerted since Dostoevsky continues without interruption and to the same effect. Why is it that the Dostoevsky type, chaotic as it is, possesses such an enormous power of attraction? It is not only because of the state of fluidity which it represents in contrast with the rigidity of many older European life-forms, but because in Russia a man has anticipated the extreme tension belonging to the type which alone seems to be quite adequate to the tasks of an ecumenic civilization. The European of the kind we have known hitherto is too narrow, too provincial, to master it. And since every forward-looking European feels this unconsciously, Russia will exert a tremendous attractive power, however the conscious mind may react against it.' (Cape.)

Those who are familiar with Dostoevsky's works cannot but agree with this dictum.

INDEX